Computer Basics
for the Over 50s

in Simple steps

Greg Holden

Use your computer with confidence

Get to grips with practical computing tasks with minimal time, fuss and bother.

In Simple Steps guides guarantee immediate results. They tell you everything you need to know on a specific application; from the most essential tasks to master, to every activity you'll want to accomplish, through to solving the most common problems you'll encounter.

Helpful features

To build your confidence and help you to get the most out of your computer, practical hints, tips and shortcuts feature on every page:

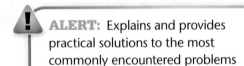 **ALERT:** Explains and provides practical solutions to the most commonly encountered problems

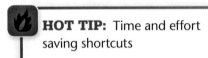 **HOT TIP:** Time and effort saving shortcuts

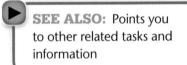 **SEE ALSO:** Points you to other related tasks and information

 **DID YOU KNOW?** Additional features to explore

WHAT DOES THIS MEAN?
Jargon and technical terms explained in plain English

Practical. Simple. Fast.

Dedication:

To my teacher, Gelek Rimpoche.

Author's acknowledgements:

Two people continue to support and encourage me through many changes in my life. I am grateful to acknowledge my agent, Neil Salkind, and my assistant and friend, Ann Lindner. In addition, the staff of Studio B Productions have provided invaluable assistance. And last but not least I thank the staff at Pearson, especially Steve Temblett and Katy Robinson, who are working hard to bring computers well within the reach of those of us entering the best years of our lives.

Contents at a glance

Top 10 Computer
Problems Solved

Contents

Top 10 Computer Tips

1 Getting started with your new computer

2 Master the basics

3 Improve usability

4 Work with files and folders

5 Print, scan and network

6 Learn word processing

7 Basic spreadsheet functions

8 Surf the web with Internet Explorer

9 Email, Skype and social networking

10 Work with digital photos

11 Manage audio and video

12 Keep your computer secure

13 Maintain your computer in top shape

Top 10 Computer Problems Solved

Top 10 Computer Tips

Tip 1: Turn on your computer and monitor

Once you have all the necessary hardware connected and your computer is plugged in, you can turn it on. But relax and be patient if it takes a minute or two for the computer to boot up. The 'booting up' routine is the process of loading system and other software your computer needs to operate.

1 If necessary (if the computer is a laptop), open the computer's lid.

2 Locate the Power button.

3 Press the Start button to turn on the computer.

 ALERT: Read the instructions that come with your hardware to see what order you should do things in (e.g. install software, plug in the device, turn on the hardware). Just make sure you're not being told to install unnecessary software.

 DID YOU KNOW?

On a laptop, the Power button is usually in the centre of the keyboard at the very top. On a desktop, the Power button is usually on the front of the tower.

Tip 2: Switch from one user account to another

In Chapter 1 you will learn how to create user accounts. Once you create more than one user account, you can switch back and forth between them. It's a simple process.

1 Click Start.

2 Click the arrow that points to the right, next to Shut down.

3 Choose Switch user.

4 Click the icon that represents the account you want.

5 If you have password-protected the account, you'll be prompted to enter the password. Type the password and click the arrow to log on.

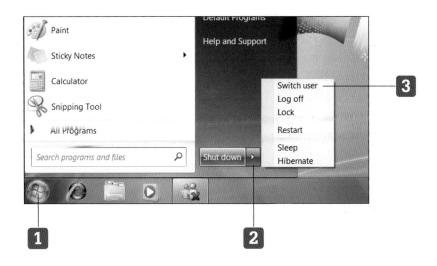

! **ALERT:** The Guest account is a potential security risk – it enables anyone to log on to your computer. You may want to make sure it's turned off.

Tip 3: Make screen contents easier to read

If you have vision problems, you can make the contents of your computer monitor easier to see. If you are blind, you or a friend can optimise your computer so it can be used without a display.

1 Open the Control Panel.

2 Click Ease of Access.

3 Click Optimize visual display.

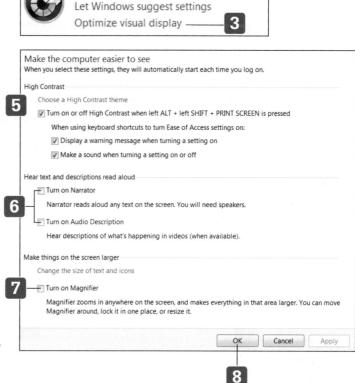

4 Click Make the computer easier to see.

5 Read and configure the settings as desired. Try the High Contrast option by clicking ALT + left SHIFT + PRINT SCREEN.

6 To have text and descriptions read to you, tick Turn on Narrator or Turn on Audio Description.

7 To activate an interactive magnifying glass on screen, click Turn on Magnifier.

8 Click OK.

ALERT: You need to have external speakers or headphones connected to your computer if you plan to use the Narrator or Audio Description features.

DID YOU KNOW?

When you choose one of the vision enhancements, they will start automatically each time you log on to Windows. You will have to deselect them from the Make the computer easier to see screen if you want to disable them.

Tip 4: Locate and open files with Windows Explorer

My daughters used to love a television character called Dora the Explorer, but here we're talking about Windows Explorer, which helps you discover what's in the world of your file system. That's a feature of Windows that helps you locate files and folders stored on your computer or disks. Here's how to use it.

1 Locate your mouse pointer over the Start button and right-click.

2 In the menu that appears, click Open Windows Explorer.

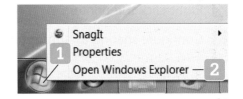

3 When the Windows Explorer window appears, click any folder to explore it.

4 Libraries hold data that has been defined by use as a document, a song, a picture or a video. Explore the library folders to see what's there.

5 Hover your mouse over any folder in the left pane to see triangles. When the triangle is pointing downwards you can see an outline of the hierarchy of folders, subfolders and files. If you click the arrow again, you'll hide the folder contents in this list.

? **DID YOU KNOW?**

When you see files in the My Documents folder and in the Documents library, note that they are not stored twice; they are simply accessible from multiple areas of Windows 7.

Tip 5: Share a printer

If you've turned on File and printer sharing you've shared any printers connected to your Windows 7 PC. However, there may be other printers on the network that are connected to other computers. If you want to share those:

1 At the computer that is connected to the printer, locate the printer in the Printers or Devices and Printers folder.

2 Right-click the printer.

3 Configure sharing as appropriate for the PC's current operating system.

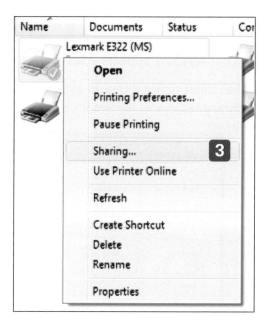

Name	Documents	Status	Cor
Lexmark E322 (MS)			

- **Open**
- Printing Preferences...
- Pause Printing
- Sharing... **3**
- Use Printer Online
- Refresh
- Create Shortcut
- Delete
- Rename
- Properties

? DID YOU KNOW?

If you click Start and then type Printers in the Start Search window, you can then open the Printers folder in Vista or the Devices and Printers folder in Windows 7 to manage shared printers.

! ALERT: Printers must be turned on and either connected to a router or to a computer that is connected to a router in order to be shared on the network.

Tip 6: Open a new document and enter and edit text

You might be surprised to find, when you click Start and search through your available programs, that you have several word-processing programs available. You might have Microsoft Word, which is part of the Microsoft Office suite, or Works Word Processor, which is part of Microsoft Works. WordPad comes preinstalled with Windows and is simple to use. No matter which program you use, the general steps for getting started are the same.

1 Click Start.

2 Click All Programs.

3 Click Accessories.

4 Click WordPad.

5 When the program window opens, a blank document is displayed.

6 Type your text. Notice that the text cursor keeps track of the last character you entered.

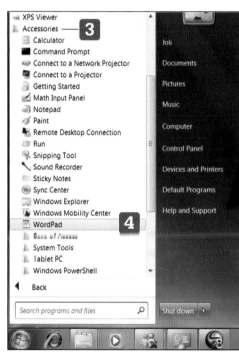

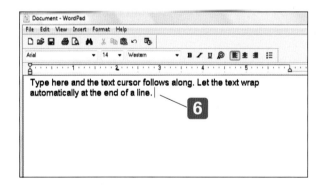

 HOT TIP: Word-processing programs automatically move the text to the next line within a paragraph as you type. This is called wrapping. You only have to press Enter on your keyboard when you start a new paragraph.

 DID YOU KNOW?
To edit, you click anywhere within the text. If you want to delete selected text, click and drag your cursor over the text to select it and press Delete or Backspace.

Tip 7: Create your first spreadsheet

It sounds like it should be intimidating, but there are only three steps to creating a spreadsheet.

1 Launch Microsoft Excel as described in Chapter 7.

2 Click in a cell and type text or numbers.

3 Press Enter or click the tick mark to confirm your entry.

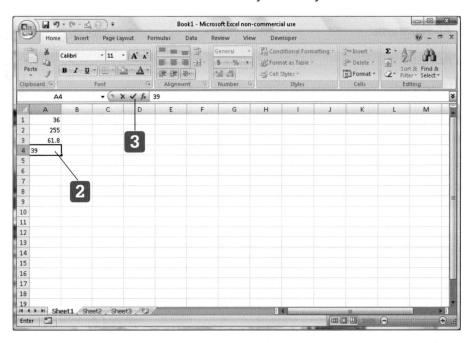

? DID YOU KNOW?

Spreadsheets are formatted into rows. Each box is known as a cell. The rows are identified by numbers and the columns are identified by letters.

HOT TIP: Use the toolbar and menu board to add and format data in the spreadsheet. They are situated at the top of the spreadsheet.

HOT TIP: Different workbooks can be used within the same spreadsheet for related topics such as household expenses and car repair costs. To move between workbooks, click on tabs that can have customised names if you double-click on the existing name and over-type it.

Tip 8: Navigate to a website

Once you are connected to the Internet, either wirelessly or via a wired Ethernet connection, you can start browsing websites. Windows comes with Microsoft's own web browser, which is named Internet Explorer.

1 Click the Internet Explorer icon just to the right of the Start button on the taskbar (it looks like a blue letter 'e').

2 Click once in the Address bar to highlight the current webpage's address. Or do you say Uniform Resource Locator (URL)?

3 Type a new address and press Enter to go to a new webpage.

SEE ALSO: When Internet Explorer first opens, it displays the default start-up page – probably one configured by your computer manufacturer. You can change this to your own start-up page (see Change your browser's home page in Chapter 8).

Tip 9: Compose and send a message

When you're the one who starts the conversation, you'll need to compose and send a brand new email. The steps are nearly the same as replying to one you've received.

1 Click New. `New ▾`

2 In the To field, type the email address of the recipient.

3 Type a subject in the Subject field.

4 Type the message in the body pane.

5 Click Send.

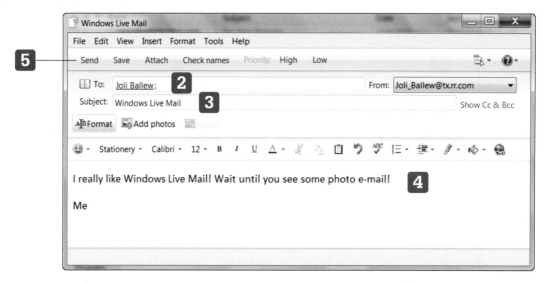

 HOT TIP: The formatting controls just above the message composition area let you format parts of your message in bold or italic for emphasis.

? **DID YOU KNOW?**

The menu bar at the top of the message composition window lets you cut, paste and spell check a message's contents. The tools let you copy text from a word-processing file, for instance.

 HOT TIP: Make sure your subject is clear and specific so recipients know what the email is about if they want to open it later.

Tip 10: Import an image from your digital camera

Anything on your digital camera can be stored in your computer. Here's how to get images from there to here.

1 Turn on your digital camera.

2 Connect the camera to one of your computer's USB ports.

3 Click Import pictures and videos using Windows Live Photo Gallery.

4 Click Import all new items now.

5 Type a name for the group of photos to import.

6 Click Import.

🔥 **HOT TIP:** The AutoPlay dialogue box automatically appears when you connect your digital camera and Windows detects it. Choose View pictures if you don't want to use the wizard and prefer browsing and copying photos with Windows Explorer.

❓ **DID YOU KNOW?**
You'll get the same prompts if you insert a media card into a card slot. This may be more convenient if you have the appropriate hardware.

1 Getting started with your new computer

Introduction

I'm an intuitive kind of person who likes to fiddle with things. In many situations, this is a good approach. But more than one Christmas Eve I've put together something new for my daughter only to find that it doesn't work because one piece is left over. Then I decide to read the 'assembly required' directions. Reading this chapter doesn't mean you have to follow all the steps exactly in order. But it's good to be introduced to your computer so you know what you'll need to do sooner or later.

Note: Although you can successfully use this book if you have Windows XP, Windows Vista or Windows 7, the screenshots throughout are from Windows 7.

What can you do with your computer?

Success often depends on setting objectives. When it comes to your computer, it's also important to know what you want so you'll know when you're meeting your expectations. If you're still shopping for a computer, knowing some of the things you can do with it will help you make a wise purchase.

1 Send and receive email and keep up with friends and family. These days, sites like Facebook are the places to go to view photos of your grandchildren or of your children's recent trips. Ask one of them to send you an email invitation. Click on the link to go to Facebook and view their page.

HOT TIP: When you decide what activities are important to you, you'll know what software to purchase and where to invest your time learning how to use it.

2 Share video images using a webcam or make free long-distance computer 'phone calls' using the popular application Skype. Click the green button to make a call.

2

3 Communicate in real time via instant messaging.

4 Do research on the Internet.

5 Connect with kindred spirits on discussion groups.

6 Use software such as Excel for tasks as diverse as keeping a fitness journal to managing a budget.

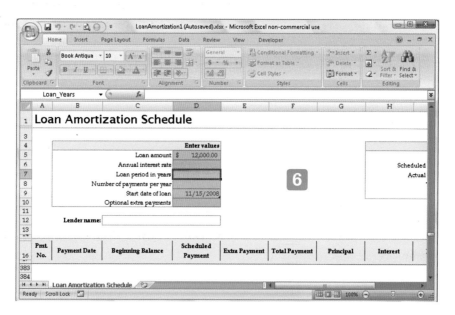

6

HOT TIP: If you plan to make phone calls online and want to do videoconferencing, look for a computer with a built-in camera and microphone.

? DID YOU KNOW?

The first computers were huge machines that lived in basements of corporations and institutions of higher learning. Now they connect ordinary people like you and me, making common tasks easier to handle.

Understand processor speed and memory

This book won't overwhelm you with techie terms, I promise. But in case you're still looking for a computer, there are some basic elements you'll need so that your computer will keep on humming like a top.

1 Make sure you have at least 1 gigabyte (GB) of RAM. You'll need a higher amount of RAM if you want to access and run more complicated programs.

2 I won't definitively prescribe the processor speed that you'll need for your computer, which is measured in gigahertz (GHz). GHz chips are constantly getting smaller and contain more and more power, but be aware that the higher numbers will make your computer perform better when running programs and completing tasks.

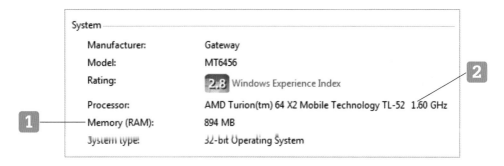

3 A clock rate of 667 megahertz (MHz) is probably appropriate for what you'll be doing on your computer.

4 You should probably buy a minimum of an 80 GB hard drive. I don't think you need the data storage capacity that is measured in terabytes (TB).

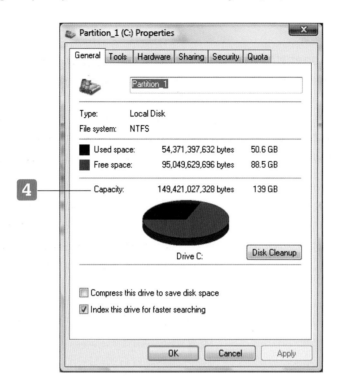

4

WHAT DOES THIS MEAN?

Random Access Memory (RAM): The memory applications used to store data and to operate. Your computer uses RAM to perform its basic functions. Chips come in such types as DRAM, SDRAM and DDR2.

Disk storage: Memory located on media such as hard disks or flash drives, that you use to create and store files.

Megahertz (MHz): A measurement of the time (or clock rate) it takes for RAM chips to make a request for data from your system.

Processor: The microchip that your computer uses to perform its basic functions. Some computers use dual processors to perform complex mathematical tasks.

How will you connect to the Internet?

It costs only 99% more to go first class, my dad always told me. That you'll want to connect to the Internet is a given. How you connect is the question.

1 As the name implies, a dial-up connection is made over your phone line. If your computer doesn't have a dial-up modem built in, you'll need an external model. The problems with dial-up are that it's very slow, and you can't use it and make or receive calls at the same time.

2 The first step to using a wireless connection is to buy a computer model that is wireless enabled. Then you have several choices. You can access the Internet when you're near a wireless hotspot, or you can subscribe to a wireless wide area network (WWAN) service from a mobile phone provider to tap into its connection.

3 A digital subscriber line (DSL) broadband connection runs over your phone line. It connects to your home via a junction box.

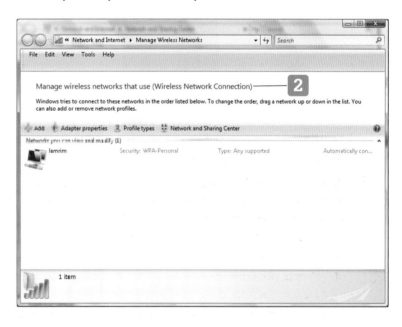

4 A cable modem, which runs over your cable TV line for a fee, is even faster than DSL. It may not be as reliable as DSL, however.

? **DID YOU KNOW?**

If you're looking for a wireless enabled computer, the standard that you'll want is 802.11n. That will deliver better wireless performance than others such as 802.11a, b or g.

? **DID YOU KNOW?**

Unlike a dial-up connection, a DSL line enables you to make and receive calls while you're online. You're always connected and you'll be able to move around the Internet faster than you can with dial-up.

Plug in your computer

If you have a laptop, it can run on battery power for a while. But you'll still want to use power from an outlet sometimes. That, by the way, charges up the battery while you're working.

1. Locate the power cord.

2. Connect the power cord to the back or side of the computer.

3. Plug the power cord into the wall outlet or a surge protector.

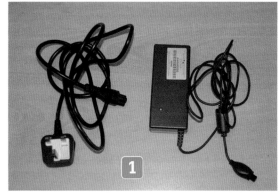

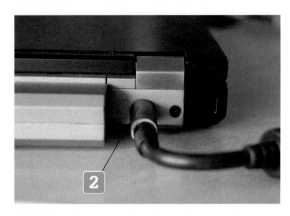

? DID YOU KNOW?

A power cord is sometimes called a power cable. Some of them have two parts that need to be connected: one part plugs into the power mains, the other into the computer. The box in between the computer and the mains is a transformer.

! ALERT: A power surge can damage your computer. It's a good idea to place a surge protector between your computer and the wall outlet.

Connect your monitor

You may not need to read this section if you don't have a tower that is separate from your monitor. Even if you have these components, they may be different than the basic instructions given here.

1 Place the monitor where desired, but within reach of the computer's tower.

2 Plug in the monitor to a wall outlet so that it has power.

3 Locate the cord that connects the monitor to the PC and look at the end of the cord.

4 Find the compatible connection on the PC tower.

5 Make the connection.

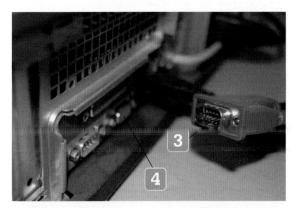

? DID YOU KNOW?
Most monitor connections plug into a compatible port on the tower and also have two screws for securing the connection.

🔥 HOT TIP: If you have a separate monitor and computer, they don't have to be placed next to one another on a table or desk.

Connect your mouse and keyboard

Mice and external keyboards are examples of universal serial bus (USB) devices. USB is a kind of connection that enables one digital device to communicate with another. These days, all new laptops contain one or more USB ports because USB is such a popular and high-speed protocol.

1 Locate the USB device.

2 Match the USB device to an available USB port.

3 Make the connection, being aware that it will fit correctly one way only.

4 Repeat the process with other devices as necessary.

? DID YOU KNOW?
Not all external devices connect via USB, but all have a port that will be a correct fit.

HOT TIP: Usually a USB plug fits one way only – with the USB logo facing up.

Connect and turn on your speakers

This isn't necessarily techno talk, but it's an important distinction: line-in jacks bring data into the computer and line-out jacks port data out to external devices such as speakers. Almost all computers have built-in speakers and almost all built-in systems are minimal in volume and sound quality. External speakers or headphones are essential if you are at all hearing impaired.

1 If necessary, plug the device into an electrical outlet.

2 If necessary, turn on the speakers. On some speakers, a light will go on to indicate they are working.

3 Insert the audio cable that connects the device to the computer, using the proper port.

4 If prompted, work through any set-up processes.

3

? **DID YOU KNOW?**

If your computer has external sound ports, you'll probably see three. Others accept audio from external devices such as CD players and accept input from external microphones. The one that works for speakers probably works for headphones also.

! **ALERT:** Some external speakers operate with batteries. But if you plan to use your speakers for any length of time, be sure to buy a pair that plugs into the power mains. That way you won't have to keep purchasing batteries as they wear out.

Connect and install a printer

Whatever you plan to connect to your computer, including your printer, will come with instructions. I strongly suggest that you read them and follow them. But I'm offering you some generic directions to give you an overview.

1 Connect the printer to a wall outlet.

2 Connect the printer to your computer using either a USB cable or a parallel port cable.

3 If a CD is available for the device, insert it.

4 If a pop-up message appears regarding the CD, click the X in the top right corner to close the window.

5 Turn on the device.

6 If the printer's manufacturer presents you with an installation screen, click Install.

7 If the installation disk contains a set-up wizard, click Install.

Install Software

The Lexmark Z700-P700 Series CD-ROM has been inserted.

Click "Install" to install all the necessary software files. By clicking the "Install" button, I hereby accept the license agreement terms contained herein.

? View User's Guide (including Setup Troubleshooting).

? View License Agreement, Web Links and other Useful Tools.

LEXMARK Z700-P700   Cancel   Install

? DID YOU KNOW?

USB is a faster connection than a parallel port, but it won't make that much difference when you're installing your printer.

HOT TIP: If you don't have your printer's CD available, Windows will prompt you to install the necessary driver for your printer by searching for it and downloading it from the Internet. When you connect the printer to your computer, you'll see the prompt. Click it to obtain the software you need.

HOT TIP: It's okay to leave the CD in the drive. That way the computer will have access to any information that it needs while you use the printer.

Connect and install a webcam

As with the printer, the drill for a webcam is pretty straightforward. You insert the CD that came with it, plug it in, turn it on and wait for the operating system to install it. But here are some generic instructions.

1 Connect the camera to a wall outlet or insert fresh batteries.

2 Connect the camera to your computer using either a USB cable or a FireWire cable. Turn it on.

3 If a CD is available for the device, insert it.

4 If a pop-up message appears regarding the CD, click the X to close the window.

5 Wait while the driver is installed.

 SEE ALSO: See Chapter 9 for more on Skype and social networking – two applications where you might want to use a webcam to talk to others online.

HOT TIP: If the webcam does not install properly, refer to the user manual.

Connect other hardware

You're probably not going to want to have a whole complex connected to your computer. But to make sure everything communicates smoothly, just follow the steps below, which are more or less the same for any hardware CDs you need to work with.

1 Connect the hardware to the computer and/or to a wall outlet.

2 Insert the CD for the device, if you have it.

3 If a pop-up message appears regarding the CD, click the X to close the window.

4 If the AutoPlay dialogue box appears, click Run Setup.exe or autorun.exe, the set-up program.

5 If a User Account Control dialogue box appears, click Allow. This may happen if you're using Windows Vista.

6 Turn on the device if necessary.

7 Follow the steps shown on the set-up program provided by the device manufacturer to install the device driver.

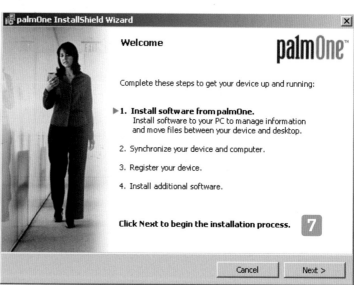

HOT TIP: If there are specific instructions that came with your hardware, follow them instead of the generic directions offered here. If the hardware does not install properly, refer to the user manual.

ALERT: Sometimes you need to install software before hardware can be connected. Always read what is required by the manufacturer.

Turn on your computer and monitor

Once you have all the necessary hardware connected and your computer is plugged in, you can turn it on. But relax and be patient if it takes a minute or two for the computer to boot up. The 'booting up' routine is the process of loading system and other software your computer needs to operate.

1 If necessary (if the computer is a laptop), open the computer's lid.

2 Locate the Power button.

3 Press the Start button to turn on the computer.

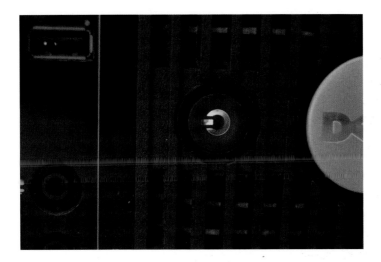

 ALERT: Read the instructions that come with your hardware to see what order you should do things in (e.g. install software, plug in the device, turn on the hardware). Just make sure you're not being told to install unnecessary software.

 DID YOU KNOW?
On a laptop, the Power button is usually in the centre of the keyboard at the very top. On a desktop, the Power button is usually on the front of the tower.

Log on to Windows 7

Once your computer has booted up, you'll see a single button for you to click. This is your logon button: by logging on, you tell the computer who you are. The first time you log on, you might be required to follow a few steps. Subsequent times, you'll simply go to your Windows desktop, where you can open applications and start working with them.

1 Press the Power button to begin the Windows start-up/boot-up sequence.

2 A screen will guide you through the initial set-up where you'll probably be prompted to specify your country, date and time, and user name.

3 Your manufacturer may ask for further details so your computer will be registered via the Internet.

4 Click the account you wish to access via labelled picture icons on the Windows Welcome screen.

5 Once logged on, you'll see the Windows 7 desktop.

6 Click the Start button and highlight Getting Started to see what's shown here.

 HOT TIP: Consult the following section to determine a password to enter if needed.

 DID YOU KNOW?
You might wonder why you need to log on to your own computer. If more than one person is going to use the machine, you'll have your own account.

Add a new password

Passwords are essential parts of many computerised functions, including checking your email or logging on to an online account. Make your passwords memorable, with at least six characters, a mixture of alphabetical and numerical characters, and a mixture of upper- and lowercase.

1 Click Start.

2 Click Control Panel.

3 Click Add or remove user accounts.

4 Click the user account to which you want to apply a password.

5 Click Create a password.

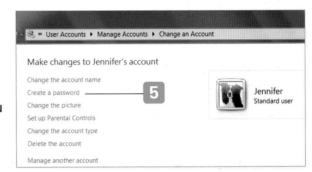

6 Type a new password, type it again to confirm it and type a password hint.

7 Click Create password.

8 Click the X in the top right corner to close the window.

Add a new user account

A user account typically consists of two elements – a user name and password – that identify you so you can gain access to computer or network resources. It's important to create an account for yourself, so you can protect your computer from unauthorised users. Creating accounts for friends or family enables them to access their own resources on the same computer, while keeping your files separate from them.

1 Click Start.

2 Click Control Panel.

3 Click Add or remove user accounts.

4 Click Create a new account.

5 Type a new account name.

6 Verify that Standard user is selected.

7 Click Create Account.

8 Click the X in the top right corner to close the window.

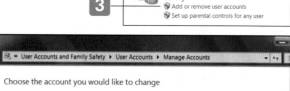

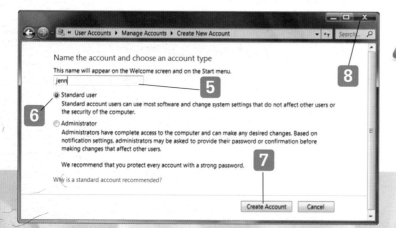

ALERT: In Vista, when you click Add or remove user accounts, a User Account Control dialogue box will appear. Click Allow.

 HOT TIP: The Parental Controls option on the screen labelled Choose the account you would like to change lets you set usage restrictions, which can be useful if you plan to let young people use your computer.

2 Master the basics

Introduction

Like learning to ride a bicycle or to cut with scissors, some things come naturally. But it's good to be logical about mastering the basics of your new computer. In this chapter, you'll learn how to start using your computer as well as input devices such as a mouse and keyboard. After you've performed these basic tasks once, you may have learned all you need to know. But don't hesitate to use this chapter as a resource if you need to refer back to it.

Activate your new computer

When you first start Windows, your computer's operating system, you are prompted to enter some information. That includes the user name you'd like to use. This name appears on your desktop and in the Start menu. Each user on a Windows computer is assigned a folder where documents, downloaded files, pictures and other data are stored.

1 Locate the computer's power button and press it.

2 Press the monitor's power button if necessary.

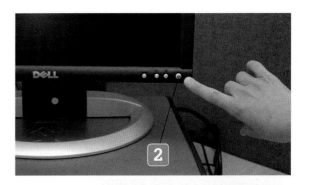

3 Wait until your desktop appears. Follow the directions shown on the screen, clicking Next to move through the activation wizard.

4 After you have activated Windows, wait a few seconds as the system initialises.

5 Click the Start button at the bottom of the screen to view your user name. It does not say Start on it but it's the orb in the bottom left corner.

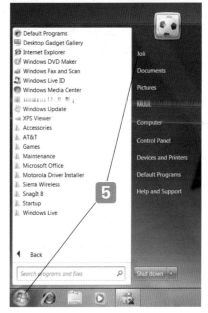

DID YOU KNOW?
Booting generally takes a minute or two, but older computers may require more time.

ALERT: In order to activate and register Windows, you need to be connected to the Internet. If you are not connected, you can use the phone number provided in the activation wizard to register over the phone.

Switch from one user account to another

In Chapter 1 you learned how to create user accounts. Once you create more than one user account, you can switch back and forth between them. It's a simple process.

1 Click Start.

2 Click the arrow that points to the right, next to Shut down.

3 Choose Switch user.

4 Click the icon that represents the account you want.

5 If you have password-protected the account, you'll be prompted to enter the password. Type the password and click the arrow to log on.

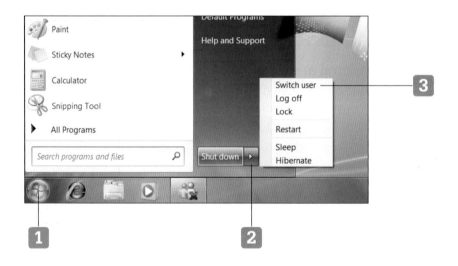

Add a user account image

Windows assigns you or other users account icons by default. You can always change the image to something else, however.

1 Click Start and click the account picture in the Start menu.

2 Click Change your picture.

3 Click the picture you want.

4 Click Browse for more pictures if you want more options.

5 When you have made your choice, click Change Picture.

? **DID YOU KNOW?**
You can add a JPEG image as an account icon.

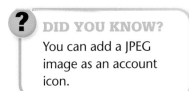

WHAT DOES THIS MEAN?
JPEG: Joint Photographic Experts Group, a file format used to save and transport digital photos.

HOT TIP: If you click Browse for more pictures, you can browse your computer for drawings you like.

Use the keyboard

Some of your computer's keyboard is just like an old-fashioned typewriter that you use to type letters, website addresses and the names of files. But other keys or keyboard features help you move around your computer without using your mouse.

1 Pressing the Windows key + F1 opens Help and Support.

2 Pressing the Windows key once opens the Start menu; pressing it again hides the Start menu.

3 Pressing the Tab key and the arrow keys allows you to move around the screen.

4 Pressing the Enter key allows you to open any selected item.

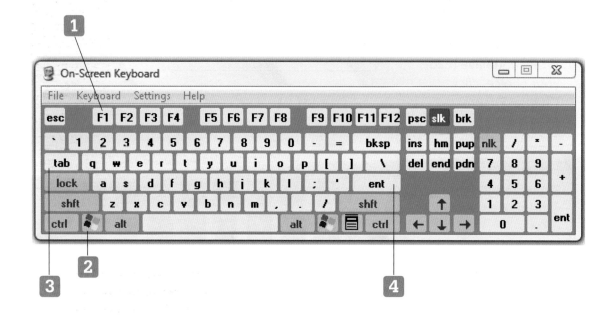

? **DID YOU KNOW?**
There are also specialised keyboard features such as Pg Up and Pg Dn.

▶ **SEE ALSO:** The miniature keyboard depicted here is described in Use the on-screen keyboard in Chapter 3.

Move your mouse

If you stop to think about it, the concept of the mouse seems really awkward. But after you understand the concept of single-clicking, right-clicking, left-clicking, and double-clicking, it will soon be as natural as breathing in and out. Unless noted otherwise, instructions to click in this book mean it should be a single click on the left mouse button.

1 Left-click the Start button at the bottom left of the desktop to open the Start menu.

2 Left-click outside the Start menu in an empty area of the desktop to hide the Start menu.

3 Click on an item to select it. (Try the Recycle Bin on the desktop.)

4 Click Start and click Pictures, you will see the window here.

5 Right-click to access contextual menus and other special features. (Right-click the Recycle Bin.)

? DID YOU KNOW?

A double-click also opens the Recycle Bin. To close most items, click the X in the top right corner.

? DID YOU KNOW?

Besides a left button and a right button, many mice also have a central wheel. Use it to scroll through a document or a list.

Try out a touchpad

If your computer is a laptop, you don't need a mouse to move the mouse pointer. Sometimes there's a trackball. But if you have a touchpad, there are buttons that function in a similar way to the left and right buttons on a mouse.

1 Use the centre button, if you have one, to scroll through pages. You can move up, down, left or right on a page.

2 Double-click the left touchpad button to execute a command.

3 Click the left touchpad button to open something.

4 Click the right touchpad button to open contextual menus to access Properties, Copy, Select All, and to execute similar commands.

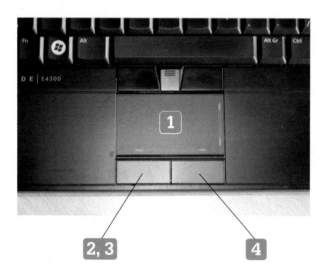

ALERT: The touchpad has a sensitive surface. Make sure your hands are clean and don't let children bang on it.

? DID YOU KNOW?
Some touchpads, like the one shown in this task, have a scroll area to the side. Slide your finger down and you'll scroll through a screen or list.

Visit the Getting Started window

The Windows 7 Getting Started window allows you to view details about your computer, learn what's new in Windows 7 and go online to get Windows Live Essentials, among other things.

1 Click Start and click Getting Started.

2 View the items in the window.

3 Click any item to view the available information.

4 Use the Back button to return to the previous screen.

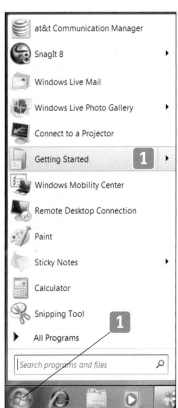

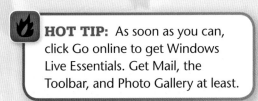

HOT TIP: As soon as you can, click Go online to get Windows Live Essentials. Get Mail, the Toolbar, and Photo Gallery at least.

Explore your desktop

Whenever you start up your computer, you'll see at least two things: a logon screen and your desktop. The logon screen is where you enter a protective password if you have created one. The desktop is where you locate applications, find files and switch from one program or document to another.

1 Click the logon icon to access your desktop, if applicable.

2 When your desktop appears, notice any desktop icons. Double-click any icon to start it up.

3 Check your system tray and make sure the time is accurate.

4 Know where the Start button is.

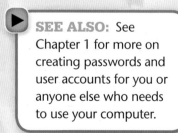

SEE ALSO: See Chapter 1 for more on creating passwords and user accounts for you or anyone else who needs to use your computer.

? DID YOU KNOW?

You'll see various icons on the taskbar including ones for Internet Explorer, your personal folder, Media Player and applications that you have open.

Locate a file or application with Windows Explorer

Windows Explorer, as the name implies, is an application that lets you browse through files and folders. Here's how to get started by exploring the contents of your drives or folders with Windows Explorer.

1 Click Start.

2 Type Windows Explorer and press Enter.

3 Click the library you want to explore.

4 If necessary, click the diamond to expand a folder.

5 Double-click the folder or files you want to explore.

ALERT: Don't experiment too boldly with the contents of the Windows and Programs folders. They contain files that are essential to the functioning of your computer. If you don't know what something contains, you might want to leave well alone.

HOT TIP: You can open this exact window by clicking the folder icon on the taskbar.

Open and close your personal folder

Windows stores any files you have downloaded, and any files you create and do not store elsewhere, in your personal folder. Any music, pictures, contacts or other critical information is found here.

1 Click Start.

2 Click your user name at the top of the Start menu.

3 Browse the items in your folder or in subfolders.

4 To close the folder, click the X in the upper right-hand corner.

> **HOT TIP:** Double-click any folder within your personal folder to open it. Click the back arrow to return to the previous window or view.

? DID YOU KNOW?

The X or close icon is one of only three in the upper right-hand corner of a window. The first minimises the window – the window is reduced to a taskbar button. Click the button to reopen the window. The second maximises the window so that it fills the entire screen. Click the button again to make the window less than the size of the screen so you can move it around.

Close an application

Earlier in this chapter you learned that in order to start an application you choose it from the Start menu or double-click its program icon. When it's time to close an application, choose one of the following options.

1 Save your work. A standard option is to click the File menu and choose Save.

2 Choose Exit (or Close, if it is available) from the File menu.

3 Click the Close button in the upper right-hand corner of the application window.

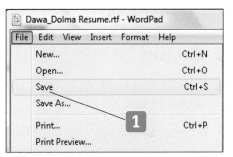

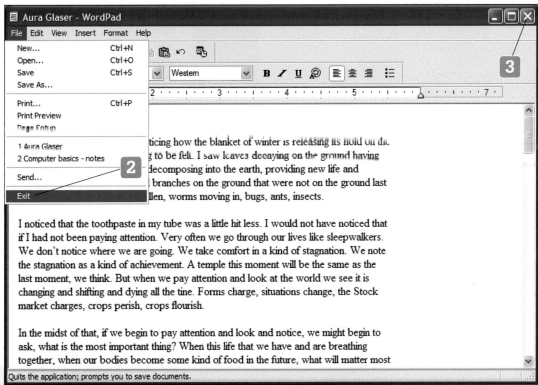

 HOT TIP: If you don't take the time to save your work before closing an application, you'll be prompted to do so.

 HOT TIP: It's a good idea to close applications after you've finished with them so you free up memory.

Put your computer to sleep or turn it off

A catnap is one of life's pleasures, so don't deprive your computer of this escape. It'll help your computer save power or your laptop work longer on its battery. In addition, when you've finished for the day you can shut your computer down.

1 Click Start.

2 Click one of these options to put your computer to sleep, cause it to hibernate or shut it down.

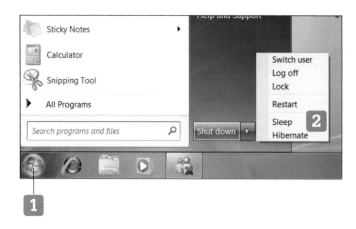

WHAT DOES THIS MEAN?

Windows 7 gives you three modes for turning off your computer when you're not using it: Shut down, Hibernate or Sleep.

Shut down: Means you turn off your computer completely and that includes closing any open windows or applications. When you turn your computer on again after shutting it down, it goes through its complete start-up routine and you begin with a blank screen.

Hibernate: Means Windows 7 saves any work you had under way before your computer goes blank. Open applications and files remain open and appear when you start your computer up again. Hibernate saves battery power.

Sleep: This mode should be used only when you are going to be away from your computer for a short period of time. Your work isn't saved before the screen goes blank. Battery power isn't saved in Sleep mode because your power isn't completely turned off.

Change the battery

If your computer is a portable laptop, it will come with a battery so you can use it while travelling. Sooner or later, you will need a new battery. Like anything else, making the change is simple as long as you know the general steps.

1 Unplug the laptop from the wall outlet and remove the power cable. Set the power cable aside.

2 Carefully turn the laptop upside-down and place it on a desk or table.

3 Locate the battery bay and open it.

4 Unlatch the battery latch.

5 Change the battery.

6 Lock the new battery into place.

7 Secure the latch.

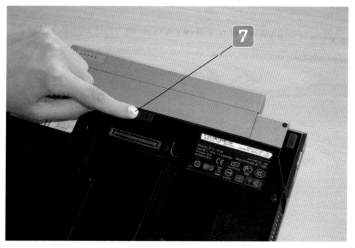

? **DID YOU KNOW?**

Sometimes you have to use a screwdriver to get inside the battery bay. With other models you simply need to slide out the compartment door.

🔥 **HOT TIP:** There's a latch that holds the battery in place even after the battery bay's door has been opened. You'll need to release this latch to get to the battery.

3 Improve usability

Introduction

Almost all my clothes come off the rack. But on one occasion I took myself to a custom hat shop where I chose the materials, colour, style and band. I got exactly what I wanted. By the same token, you could leave your computer just as it came out of the box. But why not customise it to make it yours, all yours?

By making a few simple adjustments, you gain some big benefits in your computer's level of usability. You can make what appears on your monitor bigger and easier to read; you can type without using the keyboard; you can eliminate sounds; you can track the time and weather. It's all part of making your computer work the way you want so you can be more productive with it.

Use the Mobility Center

If you need help with seeing or hearing what your computer presents you, be sure to explore the Windows Mobility Center. It contains a variety of settings that makes your computer easier to use. Whenever you want to make your display brighter, adjust the sound or change other features, visit the Mobility Center by following these steps. However, Windows Mobility Center is available only on mobile PCs (e.g. laptops, notebooks, smart PCs, tablet PCs) – you won't find it on a desktop computer.

1 Click the Start button.

2 Type Mobility.

3 Under Programs, in the results, click Windows Mobility Center.

4 Click one of the options for changing your computer's visual, audio or other settings.

5 When you've finished, click the red X (the Close button) to close the window.

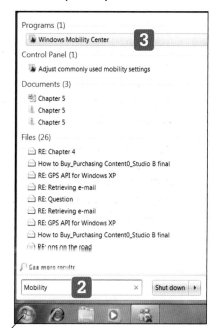

HOT TIP: Windows Mobility Center offers a blue question mark at the bottom of its interface. Click it to access the Help and Support articles.

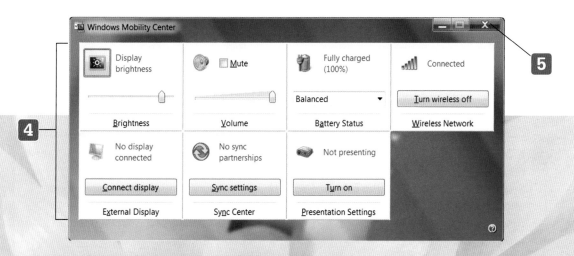

Change your screen resolution

The resolution of a computer monitor refers to the number of tiny rectangles called pixels that are contained within it. Most computer images are made up of pixels. Often the default resolution is similar to 1280 × 800, which causes millions of pixels to be displayed – but it makes icons and text small. By changing the resolution, screen contents appear larger.

1 Click Start and choose Control Panel.

2 Click Adjust screen resolution.

Appearance and Personalization
Change the theme
Change desktop background
Adjust screen resolution ———— **2**

3 Select a new resolution from the drop-down list.

4 Click Apply to change the resolution without closing the Screen Resolution window.

5 Click OK to change the resolution and close the Screen Resolution window.

HOT TIP: Click Apply to see the results, and minimise the Screen Resolution window to get the full effect. Continue in this manner until you find the resolution that's right for you.

ALERT: The Windows 7 Control Panel comes in three versions. If you don't see Adjust screen resolution as an option, you're probably in one of the 'icon' views. To change this, in View by: click to choose Category.

Make screen contents easier to read

If you have vision problems, you can make the contents of your computer monitor easier to see. If you are blind, you or a friend can optimise your computer so it can be used without a display.

1 Open the Control Panel.

2 Click Ease of Access.

3 Click Optimize visual display.

Ease of Access
Let Windows suggest settings
Optimize visual display ——— **3**

4 Click Make the computer easier to see.

5 Read and configure the settings as desired. Try the High Contrast option by clicking ALT + left SHIFT + PRINT SCREEN.

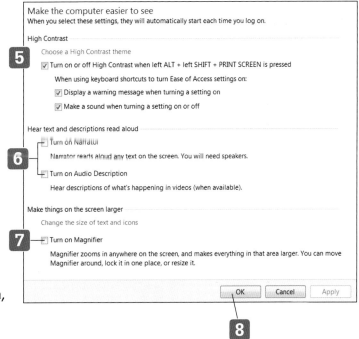

Make the computer easier to see
When you select these settings, they will automatically start each time you log on.

High Contrast

Choose a High Contrast theme

5 ☑ Turn on or off High Contrast when left ALT + left SHIFT + PRINT SCREEN is pressed

When using keyboard shortcuts to turn Ease of Access settings on:

☑ Display a warning message when turning a setting on

☑ Make a sound when turning a setting on or off

Hear text and descriptions read aloud

6 ☐ Turn on Narrator

Narrator reads aloud any text on the screen. You will need speakers.

☐ Turn on Audio Description

Hear descriptions of what's happening in videos (when available).

Make things on the screen larger

Change the size of text and icons

7 ☐ Turn on Magnifier

Magnifier zooms in anywhere on the screen, and makes everything in that area larger. You can move Magnifier around, lock it in one place, or resize it.

OK   Cancel   Apply

6 To have text and descriptions read to you, tick Turn on Narrator or Turn on Audio Description.

7 To activate an interactive magnifying glass on screen, click Turn on Magnifier.

8 Click OK.

! ALERT: You need to have external speakers or headphones connected to your computer if you plan to use the Narrator or Audio Description features.

? DID YOU KNOW?

When you choose one of the vision enhancements, they will start automatically each time you log on to Windows. You will have to deselect them from the Make the computer easier to see screen if you want to disable them.

Use the on-screen keyboard

The Ease of Access Center also provides options for using alternative input devices other than a mouse or keyboard. If you have trouble typing due to arthritis or a disability, you can activate an on-screen keyboard and then select keys using a joystick or other device.

1 Open the Ease of Access Center.

2 Click Use the computer without a mouse or keyboard.

3 Tick the box next to Use On-Screen Keyboard.

4 Click OK.

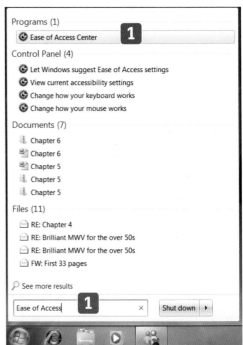

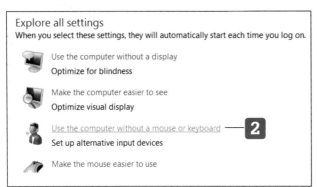

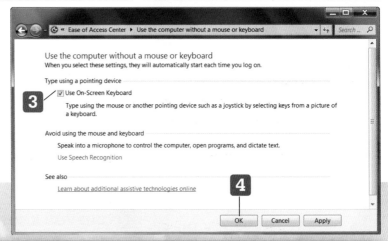

? DID YOU KNOW?

Windows 7 also lets you do speech recognition: instead of typing characters, you can speak into a microphone to open programs or enter text. Click the Use Speech Recognition link seen above.

Adjust your mouse behaviour

A mouse is one of your most important input devices – it helps you point and choose files and click on webpage links. But a mouse can take some time to get used to and it might seem that it moves strangely or stops moving altogether. However, you can adjust your mouse behaviour to make it more user friendly.

1. Plug in a mouse and see whether it behaves the way you want.

2. If the mouse behaves 'badly' and jumps around or moves more quickly than you would like, click Start and choose Control Panel.

3. Click Hardware and Sound, then, under Devices and Printers, click Mouse.

4. In the Mouse Properties dialogue box, ensure that the Turn on ClickLock and Switch primary and secondary buttons features are disabled. Skim the options on the other tabs to ensure that the settings are correct there too.

5. If Step 4 doesn't solve the problem, click Pointer Options and adjust the pointer speed and other settings to change how the pointer works.

6. When you are finished, click OK.

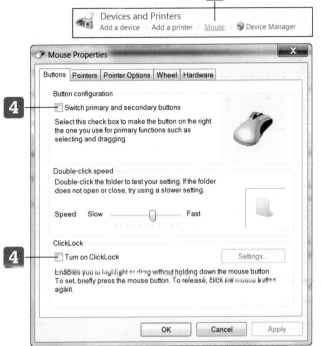

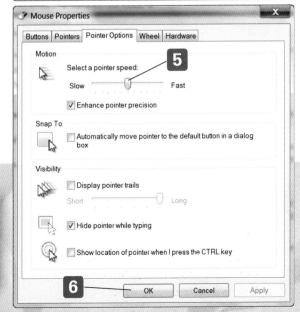

ALERT: If you think the problem is in the hardware, the next step is to call a qualified repair person or your manufacturer. It is officially out of your league.

Use the Desktop Gadget Gallery

Gadgets are small programs that sit on your desktop as icons and offer up-to-date information on things like the weather, stocks or currency exchange prices. You add gadgets from the Desktop Gadget Gallery.

1 Click Start, and click All Programs.

2 Click Desktop Gadget Gallery.

3 To add any gadget, click and drag the gadget to the desktop.

4 For now, leave the Desktop Gadget Gallery open and on the desktop.

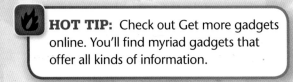

🔥 **HOT TIP:** Check out Get more gadgets online. You'll find myriad gadgets that offer all kinds of information.

Configure a gadget

As you can see, gadgets have some default settings. Weather, for instance, defaults to New York, NY in the United States. Because not everyone lives in New York, NY, you need some way to configure the gadget to suit you. That's done using the 'wrench'.

1 Hover the mouse over any desktop gadget to make the wrench icon appear.

2 Click the wrench icon.

3 Configure the options as desired. For the Weather icon, that means inputting a location, and clicking the Search icon.

4 Select Celsius or Fahrenheit, and click OK.

? **DID YOU KNOW?**

After you type your location, make sure to click the magnifying glass. This allows the gadget to search for your location and offer options if more than one city is available with that name.

Remove a gadget from the desktop

You can remove gadgets from your desktop quite easily.

1 Hover your mouse over the gadget to remove.

2 Look for the X and click it.

3 If you're finished with the Desktop Gadget Gallery, click the X to close it.

? **DID YOU KNOW?**

If you remove a gadget from the desktop, it's still on your computer. You can put it back any time you want.

! **ALERT:** It's okay to get gadgets online as long as you do your homework to make sure they aren't buggy or otherwise dangerous. Before downloading and installing, read the reviews.

Select an Aero theme

You can select a theme to change the look of your computer. If you haven't used a computer in a while or if you've only used a computer in an office setting, you may be more comfortable with a 'classic' look, where the computer appears more like Windows 98 than what you see now. If you're ready for a cleaner, sleeker look however, opt for an Aero theme. This includes, among other things, the translucent effect of Aero Glass and Flip 3D. You can experiment with all the themes before applying them, which makes choosing a look for your new computer easy and fun.

1 Right-click an empty area of the desktop.

2 Click Personalize.

3 Choose an Aero theme. One is probably selected already.

4 Leave this window open for now.

HOT TIP: Just above the Aero Themes list is an option to Get more themes online. Try it!

ALERT: To run an Aero theme, your computer and your graphics card must meet Aero's minimum requirements.

Change to Windows Classic

Even though Aero is great, you don't have to use it all the time. If you are used to a different appearance from previous use of Windows systems and you want to return to that 'classic' look and feel, you can disable Aero and choose one of several 'classic' layouts.

1 Open the Personalization window described in the preceding task.

2 Scroll down to see the options under Basic and High Contrast Themes.

3 Click Windows 7 Basic.

4 Click Windows Classic shown here.

5 If you like this look, keep it. Otherwise select a different theme.

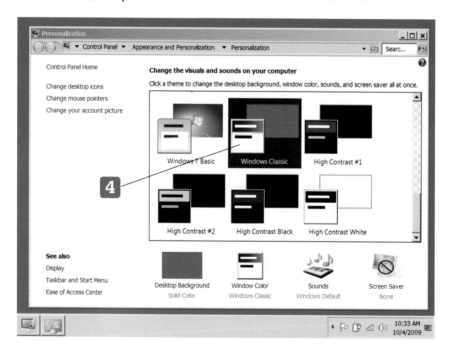

Use Flip

Flip is a fun name that refers to a fun-to-use Windows 7 utility. Flip gives you a quick way to choose a specific window when multiple windows are open. You are able to scroll through open windows until you land on the one you want to use and then select it. Here's how.

1 With multiple windows open, on the keyboard hold down the Alt key with one finger or thumb.

2 Press and hold the Tab key. A set of open windows appears in one screen.

3 Press the Tab key again, making sure that the Alt key is still depressed.

4 When the item you want to bring to the front is selected, let go of the Tab key and then let go of the Alt key.

4

 HOT TIP: The windows you have open can either be from a single application (multiple Microsoft Office windows) or from multiple applications (Internet Explorer, WordPad, Paint, Windows Media Center and so on).

 HOT TIP: The Alt key is usually found in a standard position on either side of the space bar (or on some computers, only on the left side of the space bar). The Tab key is just to the left of the Q key.

Use Flip 3D

Flip 3D offers a quick way to choose a specific window when multiple windows are open. With Flip 3D, you can scroll through open windows until you land on the one you want to use and then select it. Here's how.

1 With multiple windows open, on the keyboard hold down the Windows key with one finger or thumb.

2 Click the Tab key once, making sure that the Windows key is still depressed.

3 Press the Tab key again, making sure that the Windows key is still depressed, to scroll through open windows.

4 When the item you want to bring to the front is selected, let go of the Tab key and then let go of the Windows key.

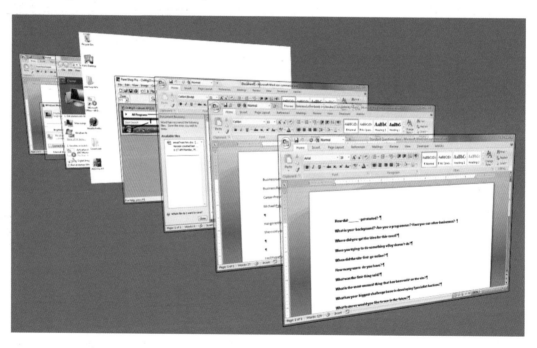

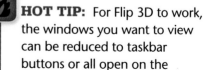 **HOT TIP:** The Windows key is to the left of the Alt key on the left side of the space bar. It has the Windows logo printed on it.

HOT TIP: For Flip 3D to work, the windows you want to view can be reduced to taskbar buttons or all open on the desktop, or a combination of these.

Change the desktop background

The picture on the desktop, which is called the background, can tell the world who you are . . . kind of like the ring tone on your phone. Unlike a screen saver, which appears only after your computer has been idle for a period of time, the background is always there, while you're working.

1 Right-click an empty area of the desktop.

2 Click Personalize.

3 Click Desktop Background.

4 For Picture location, select Windows Desktop Backgrounds. If it is not chosen already, click the down arrow to locate it.

5 Use the scroll bar to locate a background you like. Hover your mouse over any background to enable a tick to be placed in it.

6 You can select multiple backgrounds. When you do, options for changing how often those images change appears. Make your selection.

7 Select a positioning option (the default is the most common).

8 Click Save changes.

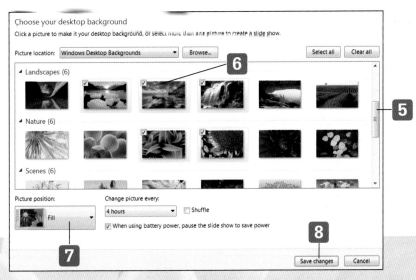

HOT TIP: Click Browse and navigate to another location if you want to add a picture of our own.

? DID YOU KNOW?
Screen savers and backgrounds were needed to save your screen from burn-in, but that is no longer the case.

Get usability suggestions from the Ease of Access Center

If you have special needs with hearing, vision or dexterity, or you just want to make it really easy on yourself, Windows 7 is there for you.

1 Click Start.

2 Type Ease in the Start Search window.

3 Click Ease of Access Center.

4 Click Get recommendations to make your computer easier to use.

4

> 💡 Not sure where to start? Get recommendations to make your computer easier to use

5 Answer the questions as they appear, clicking Next to move to the following screen.

6 Configure the recommended settings you want to activate.

7 Click Save.

Get recommendations to make your computer easier to use

Answer the following questions to get recommendations for settings that can make your computer easier to see, hear, and use.

For each question, select all statements that apply to you. When you're done, you can decide which settings to turn on.

Your answers are used to determine recommended settings only. If another program or Web site wants to use this information to better suit your needs, you will be explicitly asked for permission by that program. Please read our Privacy Statement online.

Eyesight (1 of 5)

Select all statements that apply to you:

☐ Images and text on TV are difficult to see (even when I'm wearing glasses).

☐ Lighting conditions make it difficult to see images on my monitor.

5 ☑ I am blind.

☐ I have another type of vision impairment (even if glasses correct it).

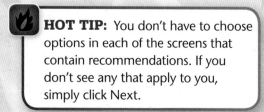

🔥 **HOT TIP:** You don't have to choose options in each of the screens that contain recommendations. If you don't see any that apply to you, simply click Next.

4 Work with files and folders

Introduction

Back in the old days, we had filing cabinets and manila folders. Or maybe you were the adventurous type who amused yourself with folders and labels of different colours. Your new computer presents you with an equally exciting opportunity to organise your materials. The tips included in this chapter will help prevent anything from falling through the cracks in your ace filing system.

Understand how Windows organises data

'File' is simply another name for an individual document that you create and save from within such applications as Word and Excel. You'll learn later how to create your own from scratch. But Windows gives you a head start on storing your files logically in folders and subfolders by providing you with the following.

1. Store correspondence, financial information and materials for groups and organisations in the Documents folder.

2. Place tunes you've downloaded or transferred from a music player in the Music folder.

3. In the Pictures folder, store images that you've transferred from a digital camera or scanner, received in an email message or downloaded from the Internet.

4. The Videos folder is the logical place for files from your camcorder.

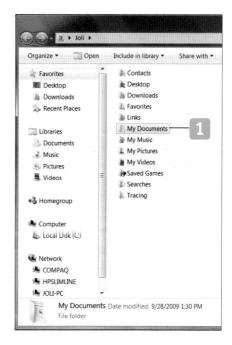

HOT TIP: You'll find the list of folders automatically provided for you by Windows if you look for the list in Windows Explorer.

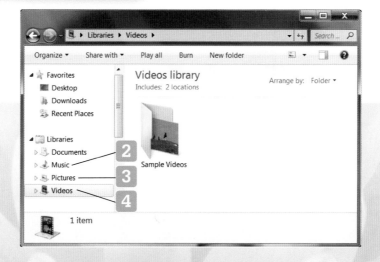

Locate and open files with Windows Explorer

My daughters used to love a television character called Dora the Explorer, but here we're talking about Windows Explorer, which helps you discover what's in the world of your file system. That's a feature of Windows that helps you locate files and folders stored on your computer or disks. Here's how to use it.

1 Locate your mouse pointer over the Start button and right-click.

2 In the menu that appears, click Open Windows Explorer.

3 When the Windows Explorer window appears, click any folder to explore it.

4 Libraries hold data that has been defined by use as a document, a song, a picture or a video. Explore the library folders to see what's there.

5 Hover your mouse over any folder in the left pane to see triangles. When the triangle is pointing downwards you can see an outline of the hierarchy of folders, subfolders and files. If you click the arrow again, you'll hide the folder contents in this list.

? **DID YOU KNOW?**

When you see files in the My Documents folder and in the Documents library, note that they are not stored twice; they are simply accessible from multiple areas of Windows 7.

Use a default folder

You can store any kinds of files in any folder on your computer. But most programs save files to the appropriate folder by default, such as Downloads and Documents. Internet bookmarks go into the Favorites folders. Folders such as Music, Pictures and Videos are intended for media files. Items and files on your desktop are shown in the Desktop folder.

1 Click Start.

2 Click your user name at the top of the right column of the Start menu.

3 Click the View icon to change how the list or icons are displayed. Here is Medium Icons.

4 Navigate the folders as desired.

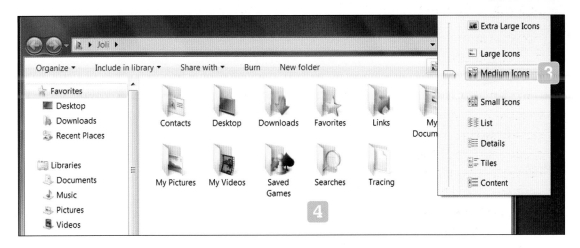

 HOT TIP: Creating additional folders inside the Documents folder organises your files. Consider making a Text folder for letters and other text documents and a Budget folder for tax and other financial information.

? DID YOU KNOW?
Although this section is all about default folders, it's always possible to change behaviour through Windows Explorer if you want something done differently.

Create a new file or folder

The extent to which you like using your computer will depend in great measure on your ability to simply find files you have created or saved. Creating files and folders in which to store them is an integral part of the organisational process.

1 Navigate to the location where you want to create the new file or folder.

2 Right-click in a blank area of the window to open the menu.

3 Choose New to list the choices.

4 Click the item to open or create it.

5 If you select the Folder option, a folder appears with the generic name New folder. You can type a new name for the folder as desired.

! ALERT: If you choose a particular type of document, the application needed to create it launches if it isn't open already.

🔥 HOT TIP: Give a little thought to names. Shorter filenames are easier to manage, but at the same time it's good to have names that are as descriptive as possible. You should also stick with only letters and numbers because some special characters cause problems when transferring files from one system to another.

Rename a new file or folder

In order to find objects in your file system, you need to name them clearly. Each file name has two parts: the actual name and a filename extension such as .doc (for Word documents) or .htm (for webpage files). The extension is not something you generally need to worry about – Windows creates that for you. But get in the habit of naming your files and folders clearly and you'll locate them more easily.

1 Navigate to the location of the file or folder you want to change.

2 Right-click the item.

3 Choose Rename from the pop-up menu.

4 Type the new name.

5 Press Enter.

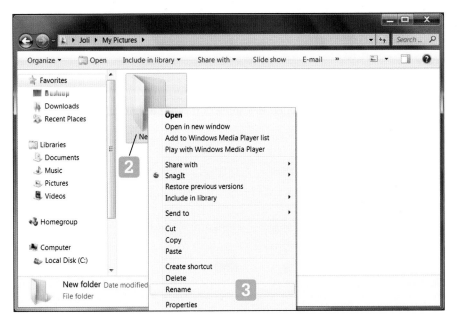

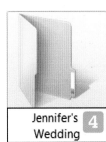

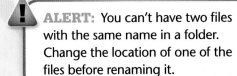

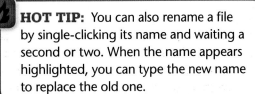

ALERT: You can't have two files with the same name in a folder. Change the location of one of the files before renaming it.

HOT TIP: You can also rename a file by single-clicking its name and waiting a second or two. When the name appears highlighted, you can type the new name to replace the old one.

Select multiple files or folders

You know how to select a single file or folder: you simply click it. You might also know how to select multiple items that are next to each other in a folder or on a disk. But there are some nuances to selecting multiple items on your computer's file system that will help you save time when you have to perform a function.

1 To select a few items from a larger group, even if those items are not next to each other, hold down the Ctrl key and click the items you want to choose.

2 To select files and folders that are next to each other, hold down the Shift key and select the files at the beginning and end of the range of items you want.

3 To select multiple files using your mouse, click and hold the mouse in a window and then drag a selection box over the items you want to choose.

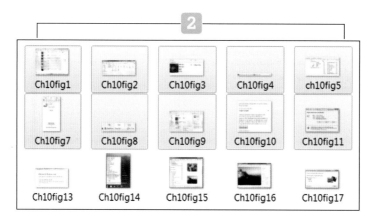

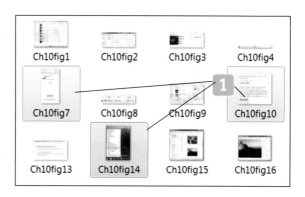

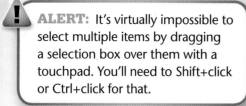

> **! ALERT:** It's virtually impossible to select multiple items by dragging a selection box over them with a touchpad. You'll need to Shift+click or Ctrl+click for that.

Change your view of files or folders

Customising makes your computer easier to use. For example, when inside a folder, you can arrange the items by folder name, author, date modified and more. This helps you organise data inside your folder.

1 At the top of the Explorer window, click the down arrow next to Arrange by.

2 Choose the desired option.

3 Above Arrange by, note the Preview button. Click it.

4 Note you can now see a new pane, the Preview pane. Click the Preview button again to hide it.

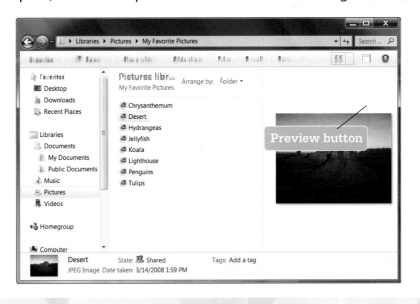

Preview button

🔥 **HOT TIP:** Note the View button next to the Preview button. Click the View button repeatedly to cycle through all four view choices.

? DID YOU KNOW?
You can set different views for different locations, depending on your needs.

Change folder options

Some families communicate in public by using a special whistle or hand signal. You can develop your own secret language with your folders by configuring Folder Options. Instead of double-clicking, for example, you can single-click to open a folder, choose to open each folder in its own window or view hidden files and folders.

1 Click the Start button.

2 In the Start Search window, type Folder Options.

3 Under Control Panel in the results list, click Folder Options.

4 From the General tab, read the options and make changes as desired.

5 From the View tab, read the options and make changes as desired.

6 From the Search tab, read the options and make changes as desired.

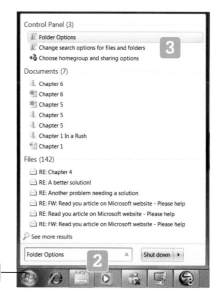

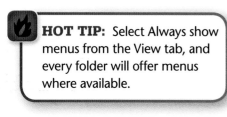

HOT TIP: Select Always show menus from the View tab, and every folder will offer menus where available.

HOT TIP: To shorten the list of search results you see after searching for an item, deselect Find partial matches from the Search tab.

Adjust the size of an open window

Comparing and contrasting is something you learn how to do when you're doing research and writing. So I find it very convenient at times to keep more than one window open on my desktop so I can refer back and forth from document to document. But then you need to know how to navigate through the open windows, moving one out of your way so you can see another or looking at something in a minimised window.

1. To minimise an open window and remove it from the desktop, click the underscore in the upper-right corner of your screen.

2. When you want to display the window again, click its icon on the taskbar.

3. To maximise an open window and make it fill the entire screen, click the middle button in the upper-right corner of your screen. When you want to display the window again in its original size, click that button (which has changed to Restore) again.

4. To change the size of a window, move the cursor to its edge or corner until it changes to display a double-headed arrow. Click and hold the edge or corner and move the mouse to resize the window, releasing the mouse when the window is the size you want.

5. Click the X in the upper-right corner of your screen to close the window.

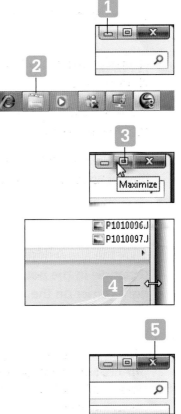

 ALERT: Don't get so carried away with having multiple windows open on your desktop that you use up too much space and computer resources. Pause from time to time to clean up the clutter.

Shake, Peek and Snap

Windows 7 offers new ways to work with multiple open windows. These are called Shake, Peek and Snap.

1. When you have multiple open windows and want to minimise all but one, click the window's title bar, and move the mouse left and right to 'shake' the window. All other open windows will fall to the taskbar. Shake it again to bring all of the windows back to the desktop.

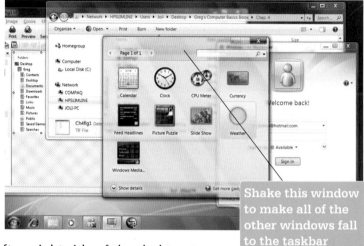

Shake this window to make all of the other windows fall to the taskbar

2. Drag any window to the left or right side of the desktop to have it automatically resized to take up half of the screen.

3. Drag any window to the top of the desktop to maximise it, or downward to restore it. This is 'snap'.

4. Click the Show desktop rectangle in the bottom right corner on the taskbar to get a 'peek' of what is on the desktop behind all of your open windows.

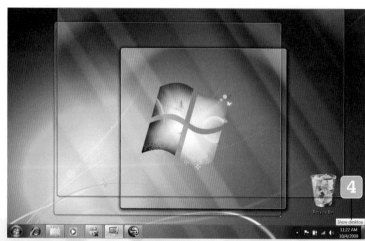

HOT TIP: Use Peek to see a gadget on the desktop, for instance, to check the weather or news headlines.

? DID YOU KNOW?
These features are called 'Desktop Enhancements'. Look for more enhancements in the future.

Permanently delete files you've thrown out

When you click a file or folder and choose Delete, it goes away. But you might be surprised to learn that it sits in your Recycle Bin until, like the binmen who move up and down your street, you take steps to throw the files out permanently. You can save a substantial amount of disk space by doing so.

1 Double-click the Recycle Bin on your desktop.

2 When the Recycle Bin contents open, scan them to make sure there aren't any files you really need. If you do see something you need, click it once and click Restore this item.

3 To delete a single file permanently, right-click it and choose Delete.

4 To empty the Recycle Bin all at once, click Empty the Recycle Bin.

5 When the confirmation dialogue box appears, click Yes.

HOT TIP: If you want to immediately delete a file permanently without sending it to the Recycle Bin, click the file and press Shift+Del (Delete).

HOT TIP: You can empty all Recycle Bin contents without having to open it first. Right-click the Recycle Bin and choose Empty Recycle Bin.

View folders in Libraries

Folders contain data you save there – no data is saved in folders without your input and direction. You can access folders (like Documents and Pictures) from the Start menu. You may have noticed that you can access data from inside 'Libraries' too. Libraries are different from folders however. Windows 7 doesn't store data in Libraries, it uses Libraries to offer access to data that matches the Library title (documents in the Documents Library, for instance). Libraries monitor (and watch for) data in your personal and public folders by default, but you can add more folders to watch if you desire.

To view the folders in your Libraries:

1. Click the folder icon on the taskbar to open your personal folder.

2. Click Libraries in the Navigation pane. Note that you have access to Documents, Music, Pictures, Public and Videos.

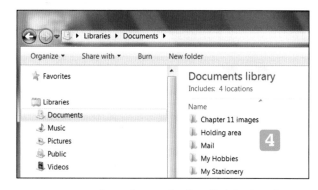

3. Open the Documents Library by clicking the Documents icon.

4. Notice what's in there. You may see more than is in your Documents folder and you'll also see what's in your Public Documents folder. You can open, save, rename and perform similar 'folder' tasks inside Libraries. As you can see here, Libraries can 'watch' multiple locations.

 HOT TIP: You can create a folder on your desktop to hold data (or anywhere else on your computer) and then tell any Library to watch it. To get started, click the locations link shown in Step 4. Click Add and browse to the location of the folder you want the Library to watch.

Open a folder in a new window

When you open a folder, a window opens. When you open a subfolder that's inside *that* folder however, a second window does not open. Instead, the open window changes to reflect your choice. Alternatively, you can opt to open a subfolder in its own window, which is a good option when you want to drag and drop files to a new location or view what's in both folders at the same time.

To open a subfolder in its own window:

1 Click the folder icon on the taskbar to open your personal folder.

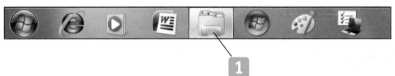

1

2 Right-click the Pictures folder.

3 Click Open in new window.

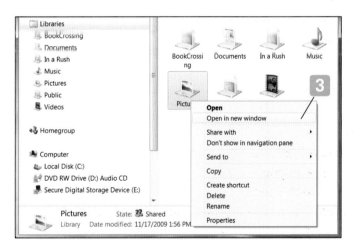

HOT TIP: With two windows open, drag one to the left so it 'snaps' to fill half the screen. Drag the other to the right so it 'snaps' to fill the other half of the screen.

HOT TIP: When dragging data between windows, right-click when you drag. When you drop, you'll be prompted to choose between Move and Copy, which is not an option when you left-click and drag. (In this instance, the data would be automatically moved with a left-click.)

Search for a file

In real time, I'm always looking for something – usually my keys or my glasses. I'm luckier when it comes to my computer because I can use Windows Start Search window to search for anything at all.

1 Click the Start menu and in the Start Search window type anything at all.

2 Look through the list of results.

3 If the file you want appears in the list click it to open it.

4 If the result does not appear, click See more results.

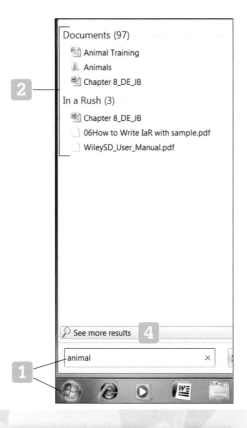

? DID YOU KNOW?

Commonly used folders can be opened from the Start menu. If you click on Documents or Music, for example, Windows Explorer will open it.

Copy a file or folder

Sometimes one location is not enough for a file or folder. Maybe you want someone else to work on a file. And having a backup is always a good idea. After you locate a file or folder to copy, it's easy to save that copy in a separate location.

1 Right-click the Start button and choose Open Windows Explorer.

2 In the resulting Windows Explorer window, notice the Folders list.

3 Click the folder (or the subfolder, if necessary) to access the file that you want to copy.

4 Right-click the file or folder you want to copy and choose Copy from the shortcut menu that appears.

5 Navigate to the folder where you want to copy the file or folder.

6 Right-click in the Windows Explorer pane that lists files and folders and select Paste. A copy of the file is pasted into that location.

HOT TIP: You can also select a file and then, using the Explorer toolbar, choose Organise > Copy to perform the copy function and Organise > Paste to perform the paste function.

Move a file or folder

Nothing with computers is set in stone. You may have a set of photos of your kids in college and then decide you want to set up separate folders for your son and your daughter. If you decide to move a file or a set of files, all you have to do is the following.

1 Click the folder icon on the taskbar to open your personal folder.

2 In the resulting Windows Explorer window, click a folder or series of folders to locate the file that you want to move.

3 Click and hold down the mouse button as you drag the file to another folder in the Folders list on the left side of the window.

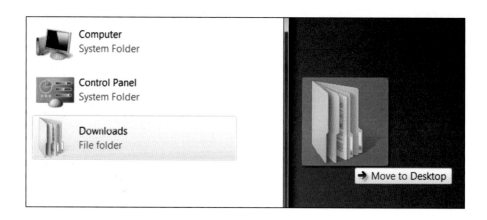

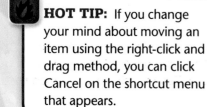 **HOT TIP:** If you change your mind about moving an item using the right-click and drag method, you can click Cancel on the shortcut menu that appears.

? DID YOU KNOW?
Right-clicking is the best way to move or copy a file. When you release the mouse button, you're offered the options of moving or copying the item when you place it via a shortcut menu that appears.

Create a shortcut to a file or folder

My neighbours don't always like it when I jog across their lawn, but I never can resist the chance to cut a corner. If there are items on your computer you use frequently, you don't have to take the long way around the block to get to them. A cute little icon on your desktop will allow you quick access.

1 Click Start and then click All Programs.

2 Locate the program on the menu.

3 Right-click the program.

4 Choose Send to and click Desktop (create shortcut).

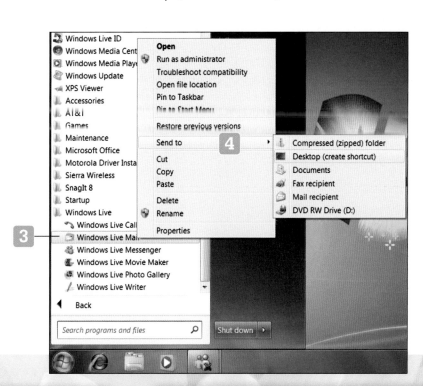

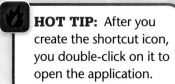

HOT TIP: After you create the shortcut icon, you double-click on it to open the application.

DID YOU KNOW?

Windows Live Mail, shown here, does not come with Windows 7. In fact, Windows 7 does not have a mail program included with it. To get it, download Windows Live Essentials.

5 Print, scan and network

Introduction

A computer gives you a variety of options for sharing your work with others. Your computer lets you print out business letters, photos, stories, spreadsheets and a wide variety of other documents. You can connect a scanner or fax machine to do the opposite of printing: instead of turning a computer file into a paper output, you can take a printed document and turn it into an electronic file that you can transmit to far-flung acquaintances. And if you don't want to do any printing at all, you can share files with others who are connected to your computer network. This chapter describes the basics of sharing your computer documents, no matter what format you choose.

Install a printer

In order to print a document, the printer and the printer's software first needs to be installed on your computer. That way, the printer will be listed in the Print dialogue box and you can use its settings for print quality, and colour versus black and white, among other options.

1 Connect the printer to the power mains, the computer and then turn it on. The printer will probably install automatically and without input from you. However, the printer software may still need to be installed.

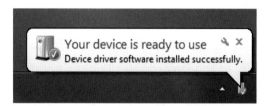

2 To install the printer software, insert the CD that came with the printer.

3 Click Locate and install driver software (recommended), choose Install, or begin the installation process, however prompted.

4 Follow the steps shown and wait until Windows installs the driver.

? DID YOU KNOW?

USB is a convenient and fast connection for printing. But if your computer gives you the option to use a FireWire connection, it is faster than USB and you should choose it instead.

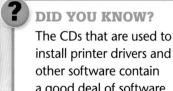

! ALERT: The latest versions of Windows are very proficient at installing printer drivers. Many times, a driver is all you need to work with a printer. Before you manually install the software using the CD that came with your printer, let Windows install the software automatically.

? DID YOU KNOW?

The CDs that are used to install printer drivers and other software contain a good deal of software that you will never use and don't need.

Set printer preferences

Being creatures of habit, we tend to do things the same way over and over. If you print most of your documents a certain way, you can set your printer preferences so it will be quick and easy. When you have an exception to the same old/same old, you can always change printer settings for that document only.

1 Choose Start and click Control Panel.

2 Click View devices and printers.

3 In the Devices and Printers window that appears, double-click a printer to see the options.

4 Double-click the Adjust print options link.

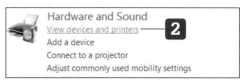

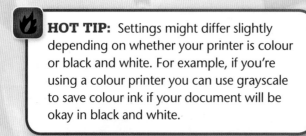

HOT TIP: Settings might differ slightly depending on whether your printer is colour or black and white. For example, if you're using a colour printer you can use grayscale to save colour ink if your document will be okay in black and white.

5 When the Printing Preferences dialogue box appears, click any of the tabs to display various settings.

6 Click the OK button to close the dialogue box and save settings and then click the Close button to close other open Control Panel windows.

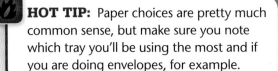 **HOT TIP:** Paper choices are pretty much common sense, but make sure you note which tray you'll be using the most and if you are doing envelopes, for example.

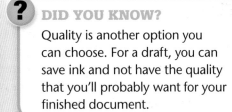 **DID YOU KNOW?**
Quality is another option you can choose. For a draft, you can save ink and not have the quality that you'll probably want for your finished document.

View currently installed devices and printers

Many offices and even individuals have their computers hooked up to several printers. From time to time, it will be useful for you to remind yourself of the capabilities of each. No matter how many printers you have, you might also need to know if there are documents currently in line for printing. The location where you view printers is the same location you view installed devices like webcams.

1 Click Devices and Printers under Hardware and Sound in the Control Panel, as described in the preceding task.

2 Review the installed devices.

3 Click the Close button to close the Devices and Printers window.

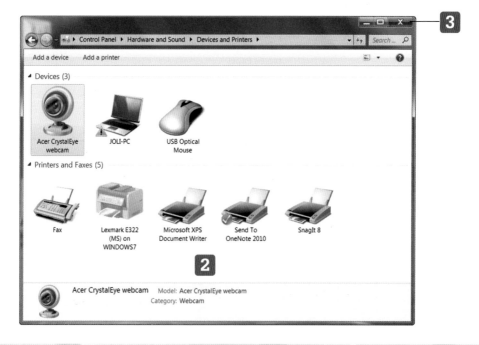

 HOT TIP: Hover the mouse over any printer to view current print jobs for that printer and other printer-related options.

Make a printer the default

Your function in an office might determine the printer you'll use most often. If you're the designer, you're probably want your documents to print in colour. If you're the editor, black and white is usually good enough for most of your drafts. You can always specify otherwise if you're working on a special project.

1 Open the Devices and Printers window, as outlined earlier.

2 In the Devices and Printers window, the current default printer is indicated by a tick mark.

3 Right-click any printer that isn't set as the default and choose Set as default printer from the shortcut menu.

4 Click the Close button in the Devices and Printers window to save the new settings and exit the window.

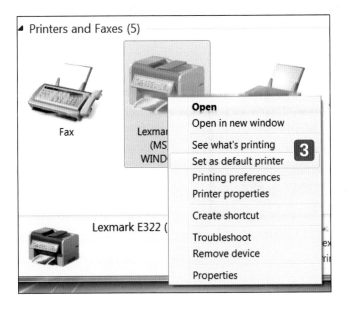

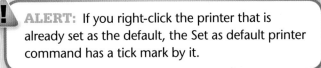

ALERT: If you right-click the printer that is already set as the default, the Set as default printer command has a tick mark by it.

Remove a printer

If you inherit a computer from someone else or get a new printer, you may want to remove printer drivers from your computer that you no longer use. Getting rid of clutter keeps you from getting confused and choosing the wrong printer.

1 Open the Devices and Printers window, as detailed earlier.

2 Right-click the printer you want to delete.

3 Click Remove device.

4 In the dialogue box that appears, click Yes.

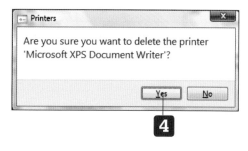

 **DID YOU KNOW?**

You can easily add another printer or device from the Devices and Printers window. Just click Add a device or Add a printer.

 HOT TIP: There's an icon in the Devices and Printers toolbar named Manage Default Printers. Click it to see printer-related data.

Install a scanner

A communications gap is a bad thing. When you buy a new scanner, it won't do much good if it can't communicate with your computer. That's when you do the following.

1 Connect the scanner to your computer's USB or parallel port.

2 Wait while the scanner is automatically installed.

3 If a message appears that the device was not installed correctly, input the CD that came with the device. You may want to do this anyway; scanners often require specialised software to work.

4 Install the device using the installation program on the CD.

? DID YOU KNOW?

If your scanner is Plug and Play enabled, Windows 7 will almost always automatically install it.

HOT TIP: If you don't have a manufacturer's disk such as a CD or DVD-ROM, Windows will help you download software from the Internet.

Format and print a letter

One of the advantages of using a word-processing application to create a letter, as opposed to writing it by hand, is the ability to add formatting. Once you have typed the text and saved the file, you can edit words and add emphasis before you print out the letter. This example uses the built-in word-processing program that comes with Windows, WordPad.

1 To format text, first select it.

2 Click one of the options in the Format bar to change text size or add emphasis.

3 If you want to preview your document before printing, click File and select Print Preview.

4 Click Zoom In to zoom in.

5 Click Print if you are ready to print.

6 Click Close if you need to do more editing.

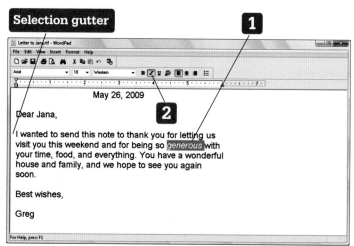

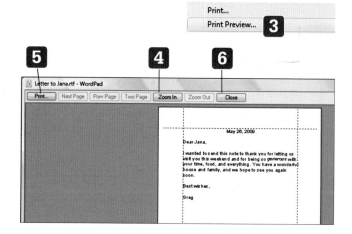

HOT TIP: To select a single word, double-click it. To select an entire paragraph, triple-click anywhere in the paragraph. To select a line, position your mouse pointer in the selection gutter near the left margin. Click once to select the adjacent line. You can also select multiple words by clicking at the beginning of a selection and Shift+Clicking at the end of the selection.

7 Click File and choose Print.

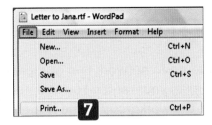

8 Select the number of copies you want.

9 Click Print to print your file.

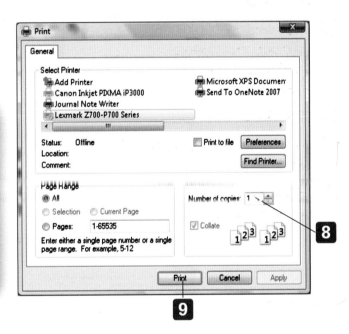

HOT TIP: If you click the Print icon in the WordPad toolbar, the document will be sent to your printer immediately and one copy will print. If you want to print more than one copy or choose other print options, click File and choose Print to display the Print dialogue box.

? DID YOU KNOW?

Microsoft Word, which is part of the Microsoft Office suite, comes installed with many new computers in a trial version. After the trial period (perhaps 60 days) is over, you either have to uninstall the program or purchase Microsoft Office, the suite of applications that includes Word.

! ALERT: Make sure your printer is connected and switched on before you try to print. If the printer is not connected or not turned on, you'll see an alert message telling you that your computer cannot communicate with the external device.

Put all your computers on the same workgroup

You might think all you have to do to network two or more computers is to connect them directly to one another or to your router. You also need to make sure they are on the same workgroup and that the workgroup name is spelled exactly the same on all networked devices, or they won't recognise one another.

1 Click start and right-click Computer.

2 Click Properties.

3 Click Change settings next to the current workgroup name.

4 Click Change from the Computer Name tab.

 HOT TIP: Make your computer name easy to recognise. It's also helpful, if you have more than one computer at home, to identify the location of the computer in the name, such as Kitchen or 3rdFloorComputer.

5 In the resulting dialogue box, type the new name for the workgroup.

6 Click OK, and click OK again.

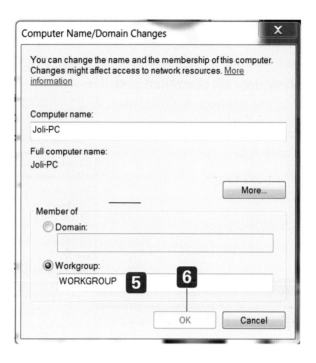

WHAT DOES THIS MEAN?

Router: Hardware that routes digital information from one device to another. It might route data from a site on the Internet to a computer on your network; it might also let one networked computer share data with another. Typically routers have multiple Ethernet ports that you can use to connect computers or a cable or DSL Internet connection. Wireless routers allow computers to connect wirelessly, as long as they have wireless cards built in.

? **DID YOU KNOW?**

You can also click the link Device Manager in the System window to resolve problems with attached devices.

View networked computers

It seems like magic. From one computer to the other, you can look at anything from photos to documents – as long as the computer's owner has decided to share those resources with you. Here's how to view the contents of a computer that can be shared over a network.

1. Open the Network window. All computers and devices connected to the network are displayed.

2. Select the computer you want to use and double-click it to view available items.

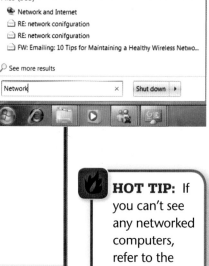

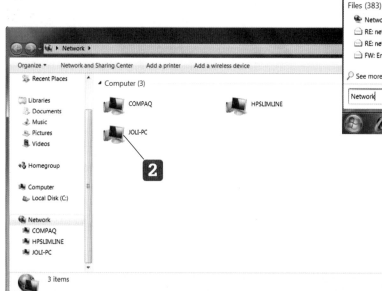

HOT TIP: If you can't see any networked computers, refer to the next task.

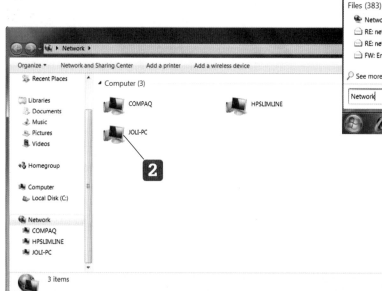

? DID YOU KNOW?

In order to see resources such as folders or printers, you need to have file sharing activated and your computer needs to be 'discoverable'. You also have to have a resource that you have designated as shared.

▶ SEE ALSO: The next task explains how to set up sharing on your computer. Share a printer and Share a folder later in this chapter tell you how to share these resources.

Activate file sharing and enable Network Discovery

To make your data accessible to others on your local network you need to turn on file sharing and enable Network Discovery. Here's what to do when you're ready for prime time.

1 Open the Network and Sharing Center. (Although there are several ways of doing that, the easiest is to click the Network icon in the taskbar).

2 Click Change advanced sharing settings.

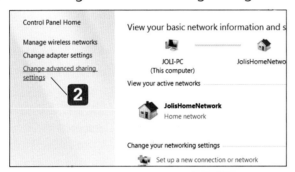

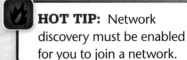

3 Click Turn on network discovery, Turn on file and printer sharing, and any other sharing options you like.

4 Click Save changes.

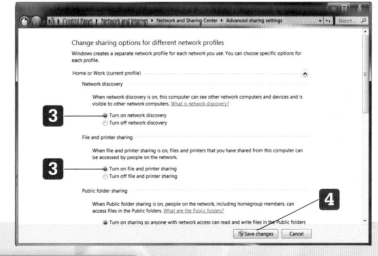

? DID YOU KNOW?

If you travel with a laptop and often connect to free wireless hotspots, you can manage that list by clicking Manage wireless networks in the left pane of the Network and Sharing Center.

🔥 HOT TIP: Network discovery must be enabled for you to join a network.

Share a printer

If you've turned on file and printer sharing as detailed earlier, you've shared any printers connected to your Windows 7 PC. However, there may be other printers on the network that are connected to other computers. If you want to share those:

1 At the computer that is connected to the printer, locate the printer in the Printers or Devices and Printers folder.

2 Right-click the printer.

3 Configure sharing as appropriate for the PC's current operating system.

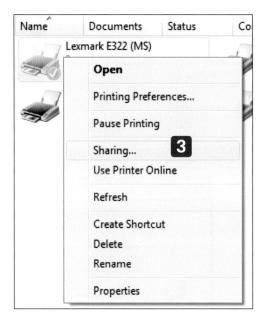

Set up password-protected sharing

Sharing is fine up to a point, but it's good to draw a line somewhere. When password-protected sharing is on, only people who have a user account and a password on your computer can access shared files and printers. If you want all users to input a user name and password, here's how to enable this feature.

1 Open the Network and Sharing Center.

2 Click Advanced sharing settings.

3 Click Turn on password protected sharing.

4 Click Save Changes.

Password protected sharing

When password protected sharing is on, only people who have a user account and password on this computer can access shared files, printers attached to this computer, and the Public folders. To give other people access, you must turn off password protected sharing.

 —○ Turn on password protected sharing
○ Turn off password protected sharing

 HOT TIP: If you have multiple Windows 7 PCs on your network, consider setting up a homegroup. A homegroup helps simplify sharing among Windows 7 PCs and is a great option for Windows 7-only networks.

 DID YOU KNOW?
Users who have a user name but not a password will not be able to access files until they apply a password to their account.

Share a folder

Sometimes it pays to be direct. Let's say you don't want to move or copy data into Public folders and subfolders. Instead you want to share data directly from your personal folders. Do the following to share the desired personal folders.

1 Locate the folder to share.

2 Right-click the folder.

3 Choose Share with.

4 Choose who or what to share the folder with. Notice you can select Nobody, HomeGroup (Read), HomeGroup (Read/Write) and Specific People.

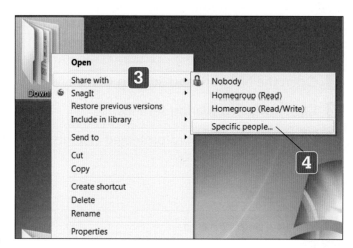

5 If you choose Specific People, which is probably what you'll do, type the name of a person to share with and click Add.

6 Click the arrow next to the new user name.

7 Select a sharing option.

8 Click Share.

 HOT TIP: You may want to share your own Pictures folder instead of copying or moving the files into the Public Pictures folder.

 HOT TIP: If you have a homegroup, choose Read to allow users to look at your data or Read/Write to allow them to look at it and change it.

6 Learn word processing

Introduction

In the old days we used actual lead for printing, which was called
'hot type'. Then we used a computer to spew out a long galley of text
that we cut into sections and pasted on a page to be photographed.
We called that 'cold type'. But then came desktop publishing. The
design could be done using software and the file sent directly to the
printer. Now you have the power to produce anything from a letter
to a brochure, all from the comfort of your own computer. What will
they think of next? This chapter gets you started with simple word-
processing tasks. Most exercises make use of a computer that comes
with Windows WordPad.

Open a new document and enter and edit text

You might be surprised to find, when you click Start and search through your available programs, that you have several word-processing programs available. You might have Microsoft Word, which is part of the Microsoft Office suite, or Works Word Processor, which is part of Microsoft Works. WordPad comes preinstalled with Windows and is simple to use. No matter which program you use, the general steps for getting started are the same.

1 Click Start.

2 Click All Programs.

3 Click Accessories.

4 Click WordPad.

5 When the program window opens, a blank document is displayed.

6 Type your text. Notice that the text cursor keeps track of the last character you entered.

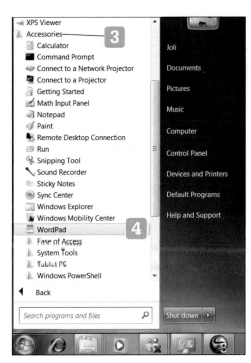

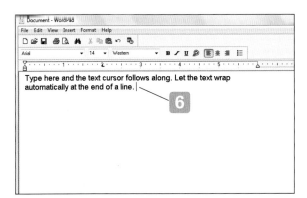

Type here and the text cursor follows along. Let the text wrap automatically at the end of a line.

Save a document

My kids and I like to watch a show called *Monk* about an obsessive-compulsive detective. When it comes to saving, it's good to go a little overboard. You can't save too often – do so every 5 or 10 minutes and you won't lose any information if you run into a computer problem.

1 To save a document for the first time, click File and choose Save.

2 When the Save As dialogue box appears, click the arrow on the right of the Save In field and click a different folder.

3 Type a name for the document in the File name text box.

4 Click Save.

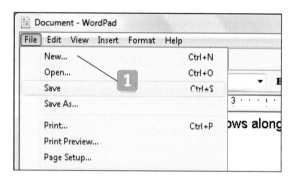

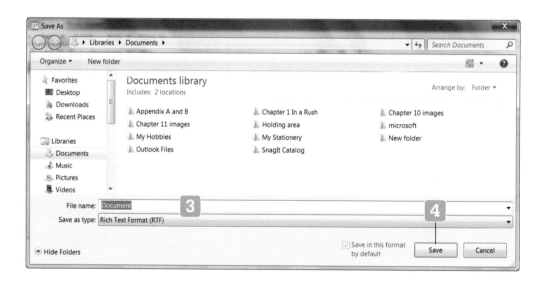

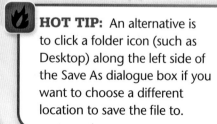

HOT TIP: An alternative is to click a folder icon (such as Desktop) along the left side of the Save As dialogue box if you want to choose a different location to save the file to.

? DID YOU KNOW?

If you want to save the document in another format, click the arrow on the Save as type field in the Save As dialogue box and choose a different format before you click the Save button.

Open an existing document

So now you have your brand spanking new document. Just what do you do next? First you save it, of course. Then you can open it to add to or edit the contents, or you can print it. Here's how to open a file after you've saved it.

1 Click File and choose Open.

2 In the open dialogue box that appears, you then locate the file on your computer or storage disk. You do that by clicking the arrow in the Look In field and clicking the disk or folder where your file is located.

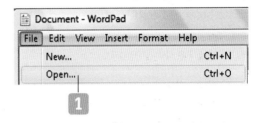

3 Then click the file you've located. After that, click the Open button.

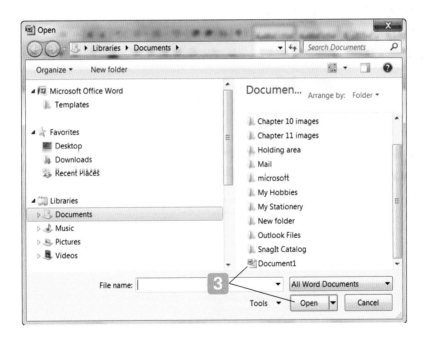

ALERT: By default, WordPad displays only files that have been saved in Rich Text Format, a format that lets you easily move files from one application to another with formatting intact. To find other types of files, choose All Documents from the file type drop-down menu in the Open dialogue box.

HOT TIP: After the file is opened, it is ready for you to edit or print it.

Cut, copy and paste text

Are you the type who likes to decorate your walls with bulletin boards? Maybe you skip the bulletin boards and cover your walls with images and quotes that amuse you. When we're talking about Windows, there's a Clipboard where cut or copied text or objects are stored temporarily. But first let's establish that you can cut and paste or copy and paste selected text to move or duplicate it in another location in your document.

1 Open a document in WordPad.

2 Click and drag over text to select it (selected text will be highlighted).

3 Click the Cut button on the toolbar to cut the text.

4 Click the Copy button on the toolbar to copy the text.

5 Click where you want the text to appear.

6 Click the Paste button on the toolbar.

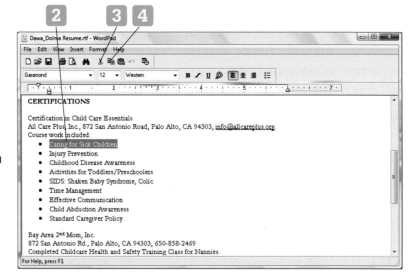

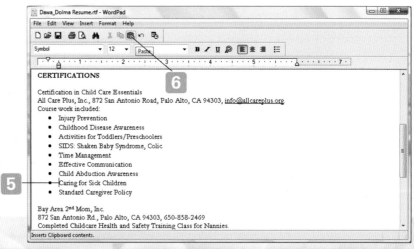

ALERT: The Clipboard holds only one item at a time with WordPad. When you cut or copy other text, the previous item will be removed.

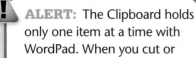
DID YOU KNOW?

Text that you've cut or copied can be inserted pretty much anywhere. For example, you can open another document and paste it there, or you can put it in an email message.

Format text

In regard to text, the term *format* is used to change its size, apply effects such as bold or italic to it, or change the font. Formatting adds emphasis and calls attention to the parts of a document that are most important.

1 Select the text you want to format by clicking and dragging your mouse over it.

2 Click Format and choose Font.

3 Make your formatting choices in the resulting Font dialogue box.

4 Click OK to apply the formatting options you've selected.

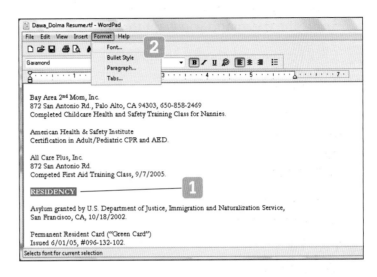

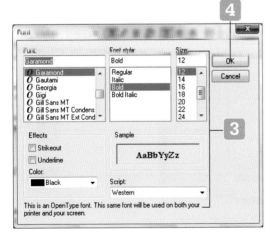

? DID YOU KNOW?

Fonts that are ripe for the picking are previewed in the large box near the bottom of the dialogue box. When you're considering the list of fonts, you can use the scroll bar to see more and then click the one you want to select. If it's emphasis you want, look to the Font style list for bold, italic, etc. On the Size list, you can make your font bigger or smaller; the higher the point size, the larger the text.

! ALERT: Too much of a good thing can be bad. Don't go crazy with formatting or your document will be difficult to read. For the most part, a page should not have more than two fonts, and effects such as bold or shadowed text should be used for emphasis only.

HOT TIP: If you choose View > Toolbars > Formatting, a Formatting toolbar will appear. That's another way to apply individual formatting settings to selected text.

Format paragraphs

Once you are familiar with making individual characters and words look the way you want, you can move on to formatting paragraphs. Indenting and changing line spacing can make your letters and other documents more readable and professional.

1 Select the paragraph you want to format.

2 Click Format and choose Paragraph.

3 Enter a numeric figure here if you want to indent the selected paragraph's right or left margin or just the first line.

4 To centre or make the paragraph aligned on the right, choose one of the Alignment options.

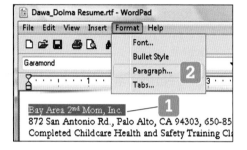

5 Click one of the Alignment buttons in the toolbar to change alignment if you don't want to use the Paragraph dialogue box.

6 Click OK.

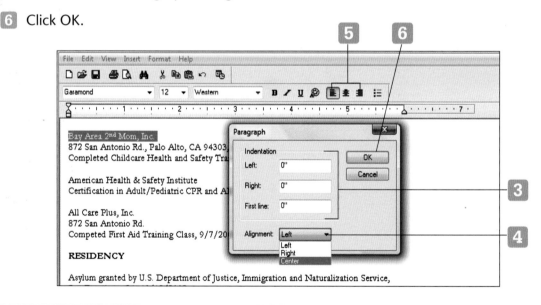

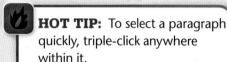

HOT TIP: To select a paragraph quickly, triple-click anywhere within it.

HOT TIP: To select a group of paragraphs, click and drag across them. Alternatively, you can move your mouse pointer to the far left of the WordPad window. When the cursor changes to an arrow, click and drag down to select adjacent lines.

Search for and replace text

When you pass the age of 50, you start having to search for things more and more frequently. If you are searching for a word in a bit of text, an electronic word-processing program will streamline the task for you.

1 Click Edit and choose one of the following:

- Find if you simply want to find a word or phrase, or a number.

- Choose Replace if you know that you want to replace the search terms.

2 Type a word, number or phrase in the Find what box.

3 If you want to replace the content you find, type it in the Replace with box.

4 Click Find Next.

5 When you find the item, if you want to replace it, click Replace.

6 If you want to replace all instances, click Replace All.

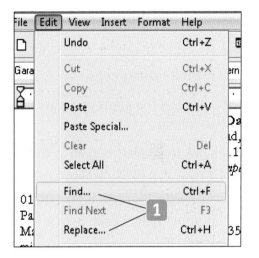

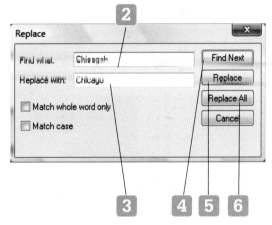

HOT TIP: Most web browsers will also let you search for text in the body of a webpage. Click the Edit button and choose Find or Search.

ALERT: If you want to search the entire document, do not select any text beforehand. If you want to search only part of the file, select that part before you initiate the search.

Create a bulleted or numbered list

Text that is formatted as a list is easier to read. By creating a list, you break up large blocks of text and you call attention to steps people need to perform, or important points you want to highlight.

1 Divide each item in your list into separate paragraphs.

2 Select all the items you want to format.

3 Click the Bullets button in the toolbar to create a bulleted list.

4 To create a numbered list, type a number before each item and click Tab.

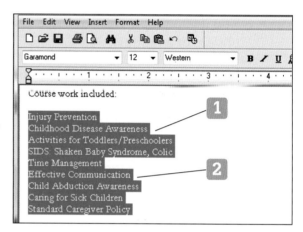

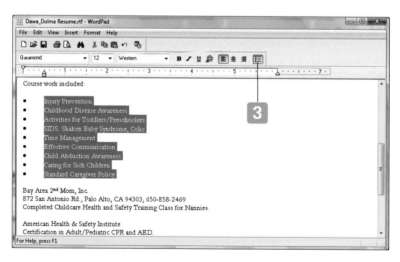

 HOT TIP: Press Enter after each list item to separate it from the items before and after it.

 ALERT: WordPad does not have a numbered list button in its toolbar; other programs do.

Insert a table

One of the most effective ways to organise information that contains two or more attributes is to turn it into a table consisting of headings, rows and columns. You can organise your information by first drawing your table on paper so you know where you want the data to go. Then use Word's table tools to create a neat table containing the data. You'll need Microsoft Word or another advanced word processor for this task.

1 Open a new document.

2 Click the Insert tab.

3 Click Table and an Insert Table dialogue box will appear.

4 Do one of two things:

- Drag your mouse over the number of rows and columns you want in the grid shown and the table appears instantly in the Word document you have open.

- Click Insert Table to create your table manually by typing the number of rows and columns you want.

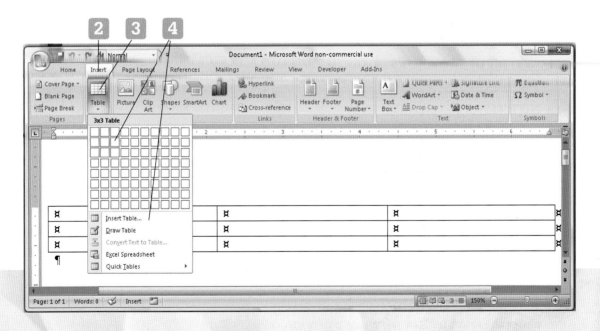

5 Click a predesigned format for the table from the Design tab and a sample of the format will be displayed.

6 Begin filling data into the top-left cell where your cursor will automatically be located.

7 If you want to go to another cell instead, just click in it so you can add new text.

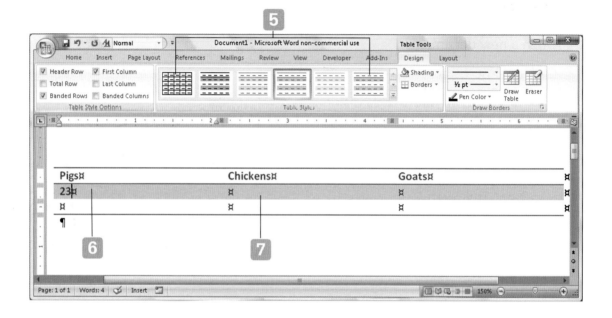

HOT TIP: If you press Tab, you'll move to the next cell in the table. If you reach the last cell in the last row and press Tab, a new row is inserted.

DID YOU KNOW?
Text doesn't have to be plain and simple just because it's in a table. You can click and drag to select any cells you want to format.

 HOT TIP: Clicking the Layout tab and clicking one of the Insert buttons will create a new row or column. Just click in the column next to where you want the new one to appear.

Add graphics

Images not only make your document more attractive, they add emphasis and readability as well. Here's how to add a photo or drawing, as long as you already have the image file on your computer.

1 Open a document.

2 Click the Insert tab.

3 Click Picture and an Insert Picture dialogue box will appear.

4 Click the file in your Pictures folder to select it.

5 Click the Insert button.

HOT TIP: If the picture file is in a subfolder within the Pictures folder, double-click the folder to display those files. If you want to use a picture file located elsewhere, click the arrow on the Look In field and choose another location.

HOT TIP: I just love those built-in drawings and photos called Clip Art. To insert this kind of image, click Insert and then click Clip Art. In the dialogue box that will appear, select a category and subcategory to display picture previews. Then click a picture and click the Insert button to place it in your document.

Resize objects

Once you add an image to your document, you can move or resize it to make it fit with the rest of your text.

1 Click the object to select it.

2 Click the centre handles on the left or right side of the object.

3 Drag outwards to make the object wide or drag inwards to make the object narrower.

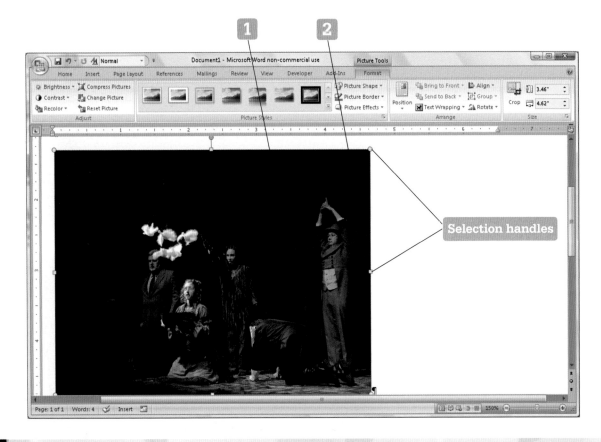

Selection handles

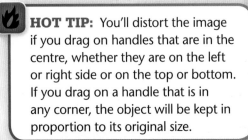

HOT TIP: You'll distort the image if you drag on handles that are in the centre, whether they are on the left or right side or on the top or bottom. If you drag on a handle that is in any corner, the object will be kept in proportion to its original size.

? DID YOU KNOW?

Another way to resize objects is to select the object and choose Format > Object to display the Format Object dialogue box. Click the Size tab and enter new Height and Width settings. Click OK to accept the new settings.

Check spelling

Personally, I'm much more impressed with spell-check utilities than I am with the fact that spaceships fly humans to the moon. This is a scientific advance that really has changed the world for the better. If you follow the first steps below and no discernable errors are in the text, a message appears that the spell check is complete. This task uses Microsoft Word as an example.

1 Open the document that needs to be spell checked.

2 Click the Review tab.

3 Click Spelling & Grammar.

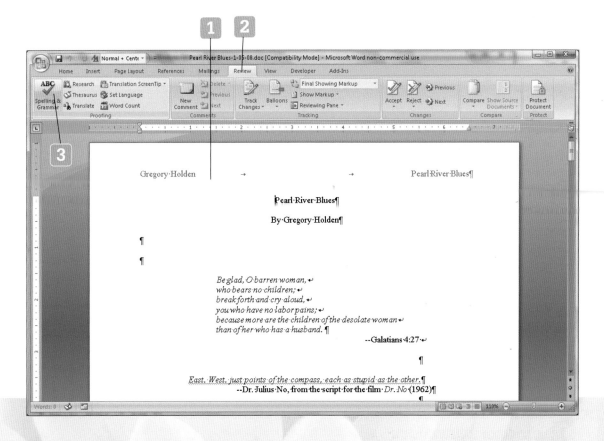

HOT TIP: In addition to checking spelling, Works allows you to select the Check Grammar tick box in the Spelling & Grammar dialogue box. Then Works will display sentences with possible grammatical problems and give you suggestions for how to fix them.

4 Choose your action from the dialogue box that appears.

5 When the Spell Checker moves to the next word that may be misspelled, repeat the previous direction.

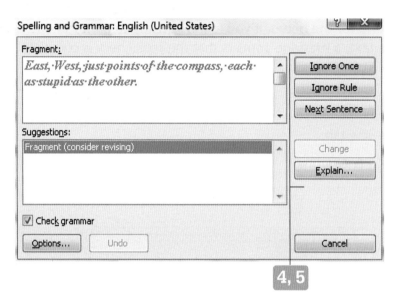

4, 5

6 Spell Checker will indicate that the spell check is complete by presenting you with the Close box.

7 Click Close to close the dialogue box.

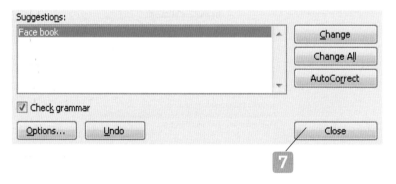

7

? DID YOU KNOW?

If you use a lot of acronyms, proper names or scientific terms, you need to stop Works from telling you over and over again that these words are misspelled. Use the Add feature to put these words in the dictionary so Works will skip them.

Change page set-up

Before you print a file, you should know how to change the default page set-up. You can control settings such as margins and page orientation. You can do that when you create the document or you can wait until you're ready to print the document. This task uses WordPad as an example.

1　Open the document.

2　Click File.

3　Choose Page Setup.

4　Also specify the size of the paper you will print to and select the source for the paper if necessary.

5　In the Page Setup dialogue box that appears, type new values for the margins you want to change.

6　Choose either Portrait or Landscape.

7　Click OK.

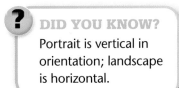

? DID YOU KNOW?

Portrait is vertical in orientation; landscape is horizontal.

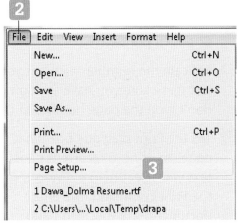

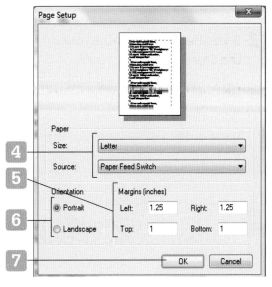

 HOT TIP: To insert headers or footers in your document, look for the command on the View menu. Then you can tick settings in the dialogue box to, for example, specify how far from the edge of the paper the header or footer should appear.

Print a document

If you've used computers at all before, you're familiar with the basic print choices. If not, you'll be happy to know that you can exercise a good deal of control over printing. You can limit the number of pages you want to print, or zoom in and out, for instance.

1 Click File and choose Print.

2 Choose a printer.

3 Indicate the number of copies you want to print. Just make sure you have enough paper and that you don't type the page number in this space.

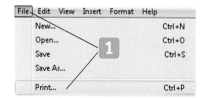

4 Tell the Print dialogue box what pages to print: the current page, text you select before giving the Print command, the entire document or a specified page or range of pages.

5 If you need to assemble your documents yourself, you'll appreciate the collating function that will assemble sets of documents in the correct page order.

6 Click Print.

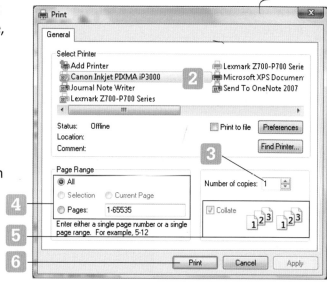

![4]
![5]
![6]

⚠️ **ALERT:** Most programs will let you click the Print icon in the toolbar. But be careful: you may send the file directly to the printer without being able to adjust the number of copies or other settings.

▶ **SEE ALSO:** Before you can print, you need to install your printer software, as described in Install a printer in Chapter 5.

❓ **DID YOU KNOW?**

The selection of print options you have depends on the program you are using as well as your printer. What you see here may look different on your computer.

7 Basic spreadsheet functions

Introduction

Like boys and girls, text and numbers are different. A format that is lovely for words by definition isn't the best way to manipulate numbers. That's why your higher power invented spreadsheets. Some people take to them like ducks to water. Others find that they take some getting used to. But I promise that the concepts in this chapter are easier to implement than, in some cases, to read. Just take a deep breath, hold your nose and jump right in. The water will be fine.

Start Excel

Excel gives you a head start by providing you with several ways to hit the ground running. You decide which way is more to your liking. In any case, you'll get a blank workbook where you can begin working immediately. You'll have to find your own excuse to procrastinate.

1 Click the Start button on the taskbar.

2 Point to All Programs.

3 Click Microsoft Office.

4 Click Microsoft Office Excel 2007.

5 Follow the instructions to complete the process if Microsoft Office asks you to activate the program

---

? **DID YOU KNOW?**

Double-clicking any Excel workbook icon in Windows Explorer opens that file and Excel. Or you can create a program shortcut from the Start menu to the desktop. Click the Start menu, point to All Programs, click Microsoft Office, right-click Microsoft Office Excel 2007, point to Send to, then click Desktop (create shortcut).

HOT TIP: To activate Microsoft Office later, click the Office button, click Excel Options, click Resources, then click Activate. If a Privacy dialogue box appears, select the options you want, then click OK.

Create your first spreadsheet

It sounds like it should be intimidating, but there are only three steps to creating a spreadsheet.

1 Launch Microsoft Excel as described in the preceding task.

2 Click in a cell and type text or numbers.

3 Press Enter or click the tick mark to confirm your entry.

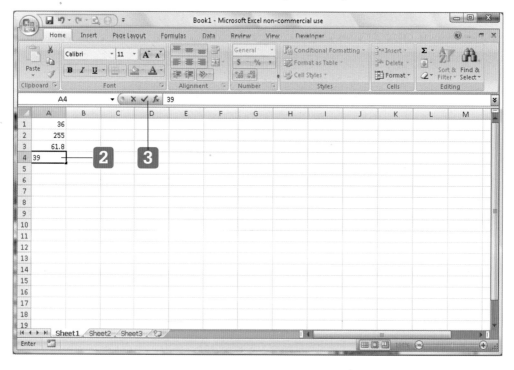

HOT TIP: Use the toolbar and menu board to add and format data in the spreadsheet. They are situated at the top of the spreadsheet.

? DID YOU KNOW?

Spreadsheets are formatted into rows. Each box is known as a cell. The rows are identified by numbers and the columns are identified by letters.

HOT TIP: Different workbooks can be used within the same spreadsheet for related topics such as household expenses and car repair costs. To move between workbooks, click on tabs that can have customised names if you double-click on the existing name and over-type it.

Open an existing workbook

If you want to open an existing workbook, you have two choices. You can double-click the icon for the workbook you want to open and, if Excel isn't running already, it will start up and open the file simultaneously. If Excel is already running, another option is to follow the steps below.

1 Click the Office button.

2 Click a recently used workbook if it appears on the list.

3 As an alternative, or if the workbook does not appear on the list, click Open.

4 If the file is located in another folder, click one of the down arrows and then navigate to the file.

5 Alternatively, locate the folder that contains the file in the Folders list.

6 Click the file name to select it.

7 Click Open.

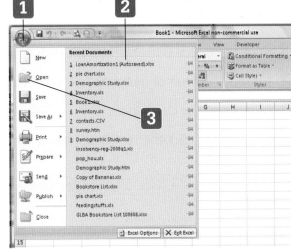

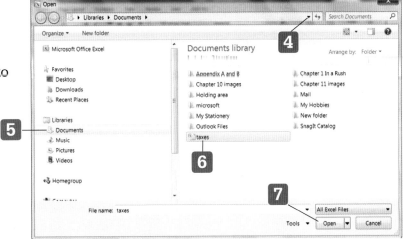

HOT TIP: If you want a specific file type, click the Files of type list arrow and choose whatever meets your needs.

? DID YOU KNOW?

Click the pin icon next to the name of a file in the Recent Documents list to pin it to the list. It remains there until you click the pin icon again to unpin it.

Create a workbook from a template

There is an Excel workbook file that you can use to get a unified work design. You will find sets of worksheets and themes that are already designed. The text and graphics are all you have to come up with.

1 Click the Office button and then click New.

2 Choose the type of template you want from the Templates.

3 Click Create or Download.

4 If necessary, click the template, then click OK.

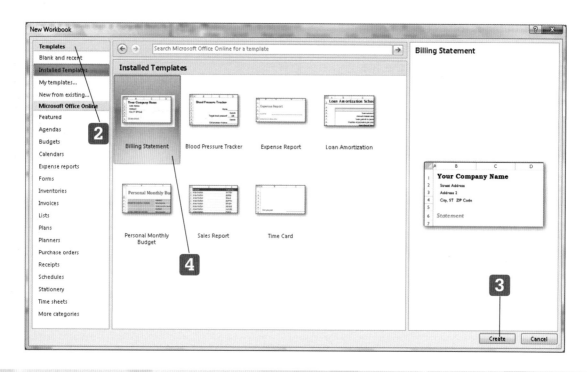

? **DID YOU KNOW?**

When you know what you want to say but need help in making it look good, go to www.microsoft.com, click the Office link, then search for Excel Templates. Lists of categories will help you find what you want. Or check out the Spotlight section in the Featured category (you can set it to automatically update). Excel has conveniently also installed a number of templates you can use without going anywhere.

Select a cell

Once you have a cell, you obviously will want to do something with it. Maybe you will enter data in it, edit or move it, or perform an action. But first you need to select it so it becomes the active cell. If you want to work with a group of cells, however, you need to first select them as a range. It's not necessary for them to be contiguous (adjacent to each other); they can be non-contiguous (in different parts of the worksheet).

1 To select a contiguous range, click the first cell that you want to include in the range.

2 Drag the mouse to the last cell that you want to include in the range (or hold down the Shift key and then click the lower-right cell in the range instead of dragging).

3 To select a non-contiguous range, repeat steps 1 and 2 above if necessary. Then press and hold Ctrl, then click the next cell (or drag the pointer over the next group of cells you want in the range).

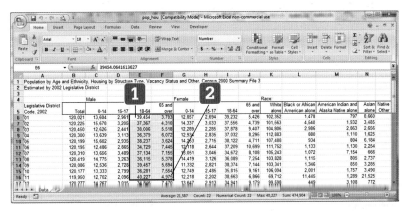

4 Repeat step 3 until all non-contiguous ranges are selected.

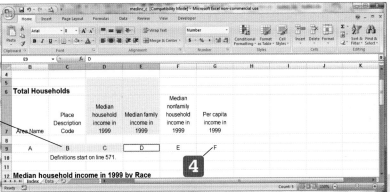

Select rows, columns and ranges

In some cases you'll want to select rows or columns. Or you may want to select a range of cells across multiple worksheets. Types of data that can be in a cell include comments, constants, formulas or conditional formats. Use the Go To Special dialogue box to help you find what you're looking for.

1 If you need only one row or column, click in its heading or select any cell it contains. Then press Shift+space bar.

2 If you need more than one row or column but the ones you want are next to each other, drag in the row or column heading.

3 Sometimes you need more than one row or column but the ones you want aren't next to each other. In that case, press Ctrl while you click the borders for the rows or columns you want to include.

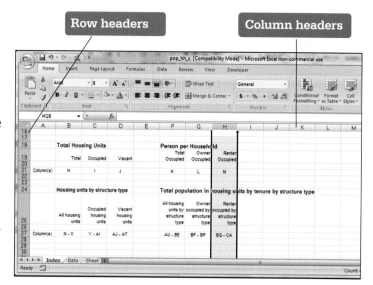

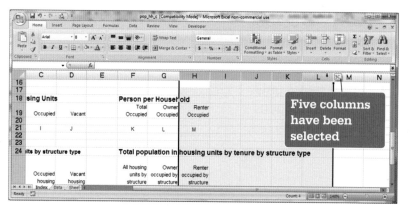

Enter a label

Labels create a report that makes sense. Otherwise you'd just have a worksheet full of meaningless numbers. In other words, they describe the data in worksheet cells, columns and rows.

1 To enter a text label, click a cell and then type your label.

2 Press Enter, or click the Enter button on the formula bar (which looks like a tick).

3 To enter a number as a label, click a cell where you want to enter a number as a label.

4 Type an apostrophe, then type a number value.

5 Press Enter or click the Enter button on the formula bar.

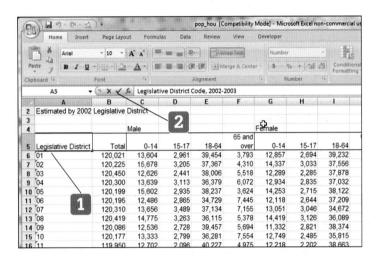

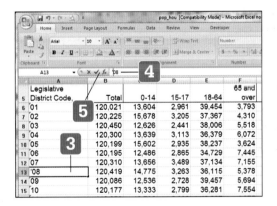

HOT TIP: Using Excel's AutoComplete feature will keep your labels consistent. However, you can't use it for numbers, dates or times. It automatically completes your entries based on labels you've done before. Keep typing if you want something other than what it comes up with at first. When you're happy, press Enter or click the Enter button on the formula bar.

? DID YOU KNOW?

Why do you need to type an apostrophe on a number label? It's what keeps Excel from using the number in its calculations. The apostrophe is just a label prefix that won't appear on the worksheet.

Enter a value

A value can be a whole number, decimal, percentage or date. You can enter it using the numbers on the top row of your keyboard or by pressing your Num Lock key – that's the numeric keypad on the right.

1 To enter a value, click your chosen cell.

2 Type a value.

3 Press Enter or click the Enter button on the formula bar.

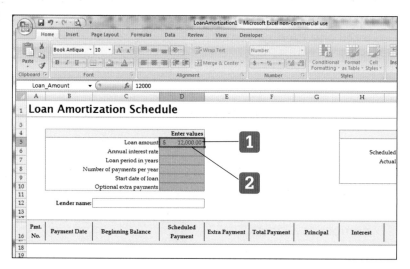

4 Type a date using a slash or a hyphen between the month, day and year in a cell or on the formula bar. Type an hour based on a 12-hour clock, followed by a colon, followed by the minute, followed by a space and ending with an 'a' (for a.m.) or a 'p' (for p.m.).

5 Press Enter or click the Enter button on the formula bar.

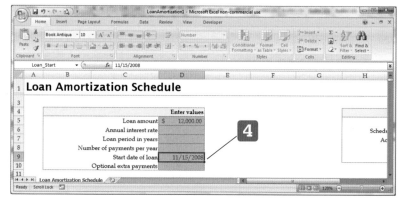

 DID YOU KNOW?

Excel will change the cell's format to a default date or time format. Or Excel can customise the way values, dates or times of day are shown.

 HOT TIP: More simple is better when it comes to data entries. Instead of typing '50.00', just type '50'.

 HOT TIP: What do you use to format your cell entries with decimal places, commas, dollar signs and other attributes? That's the Number format list arrow.

Select and name a worksheet

When you work with Excel, you store and analyse values on individual sections of workbooks called 'worksheets' or 'sheets'. Each time you open a new workbook, you'll automatically see three worksheets. The names you'll be given are Sheet1, Sheet2 and Sheet3. But you should choose your own name as you create a worksheet so that you can remember what's in it. That way, you'll know which sheet to choose when you're faced with a set of sheets. The one you're working on is the 'active' or 'selected' worksheet. When you select the entire worksheet, changes you make are applied throughout. The tab is like a file folder label.

1 If necessary, display other tabs by clicking a sheet tab and hitting the scroll button.

2 To make the worksheet active, click a sheet tab.

3 To select several worksheets, press and hold CTRL as you click other sheet tabs. [Group] will then appear in the title bar.

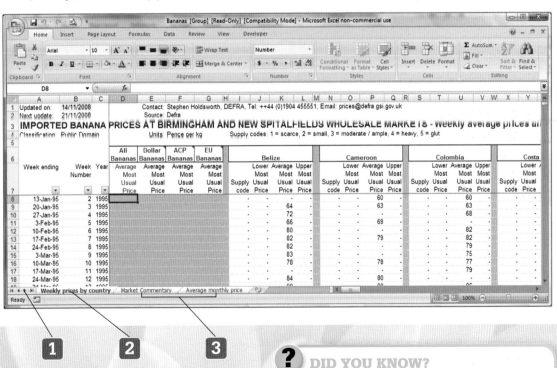

DID YOU KNOW?

If you want to be able to see a lot of sheet tabs, pick short names. The sheet tab will be bigger when the name is big.

4 To name a sheet, double-click the sheet tab. Or you can click the Home tab, click the Format button, then click Rename.

5 Type the name you've chosen.

6 Press Enter.

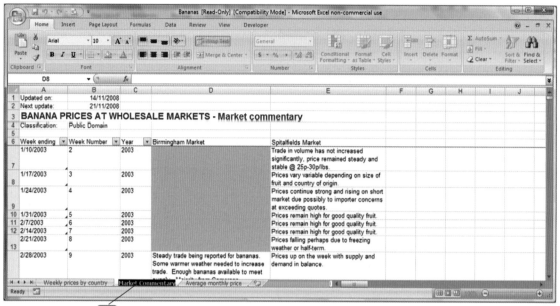

5

🔥 **HOT TIP:** To select all the worksheets, right-click any sheet tab and then click Select all sheets.

❓ **DID YOU KNOW?**

If you need more than three worksheets for your project, add them at this point. That way you'll have all the information you need for your project in one file.

Format numbers

Numeric formats can be applied to numbers to better reflect the type of information they represent. That way the appearance of the data in the cells of a worksheet can be changed without changing the actual value in the cell.

1 Find the number(s) you want to format. Then select the cell or range they are in.

2 Click the Home tab.

3 Click the Number format list arrow. Then choose a format.

4 To tweak the format, click a format button.

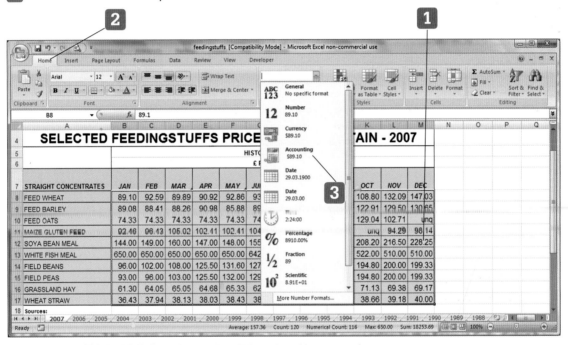

? DID YOU KNOW?

You can apply more than one attribute to the range.

🔥 HOT TIP: Numbers can be formatted in currencies from different countries. In the Format Cells dialogue box, click the Number tab, click Currency in the Category list, click the Symbol list arrow, then click an international currency symbol.

? DID YOU KNOW?

To turn on and off the buttons on the Home tab ribbon and mini-toolbar, just click on them.

Perform simple calculations

If you need to perform a calculation just to get a preview of a result, you can do so with the status bar. It can display the sum, average, maximum, minimum or count of selected values. That may be more simple than using a formula to accomplish such a task.

1 Select the cell or range you want to calculate. The sum, average and count of the selected cells appear in the status bar.

2 If you need to see the maximum, minimum or other result, right-click the status bar.

3 Click an option in the context menu to toggle it on or off.

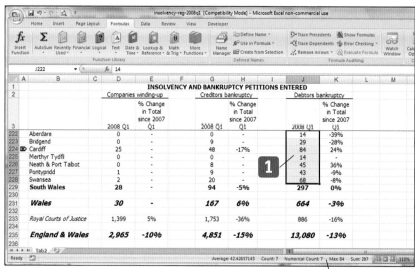

Calculations appear here

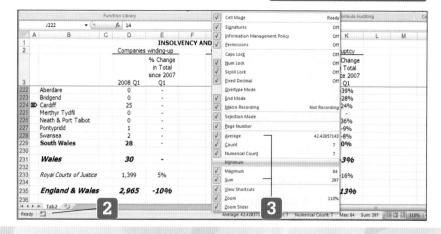

! **ALERT:** Don't be alarmed if you don't see the results in the worksheet when they are printed. That doesn't happen when you use the status bar for a calculation.

8 Surf the web with Internet Explorer

Introduction

Just as interstate highways changed the transportation landscape, the World Wide Web became the information superhighway. But there are rules of the road that apply when you're zooming across the country, and there are also protocols that keep you safe and on course as you cruise online. Your prime navigator for your journey across cyberspace is a program that comes built in with Windows, Microsoft's web browser, Internet Explorer.

In this chapter you'll learn all the basics you need to get online and surf the Web with Internet Explorer. You'll also learn some shortcuts that will help you revisit your favourite websites easily or visit several sites at once. Have a wonderful trip!

Find a connection to the Internet

When you're standing in the supermarket aisle wondering what cereal to buy, first you have to decide whether you'd rather have granola or oatmeal for breakfast. If you're in the mood for oatmeal, you then have to compare brands to determine which is the best choice for you. If you are apt to oversleep, instant would be quicker to zap in the microwave than the kind you cook in a pan on the stove. But if you're trying to save money, the old-fashioned kind might be cheaper. Or you may be looking for convenience and not willing to wash the pan. Or maybe you don't have a microwave or are looking for something to cook at a campsite while travelling. When selecting an Internet Service Provider (ISP), you also need to consider access, cost, convenience and equipment.

1 If you already have cable television, you can add high-speed Internet. Ask your provider for the additional monthly cost.

2 If you already have a mobile phone service, ask your mobile provider if you can get online with your laptop using their mobile broadband service. You would get a wireless card for your laptop that can get online from anywhere you have coverage.

3 Visit a site like Broadband-Finder (www.broadband-finder.co.uk) to compare prices for obtaining your own new Internet service.

? DID YOU KNOW?

If you want to connect from anywhere, consider a wireless (satellite) provider or a mobile phone provider such as T-Mobile. If you'll only be using your computer at home, look into a cable connection (broadband or DSL); if you don't have access to broadband, you'll have to acquire a lot of patience with a wireless or dial-up connection using your phone line.

HOT TIP: If you already have a mobile phone, TV cable or satellite TV provider, ask about bundled pricing. Otherwise negotiate with your new ISP based on how often you go online and how much bandwidth you use by sending and receiving data.

Obtain the proper settings

My parents named their bouncing new baby boy Gregory, but once I signed up with an ISP I got a whole new group of names. The good news is that I got to pick them out for myself; the bad news is that, unlike Greg, I had to make a special effort to remember them.

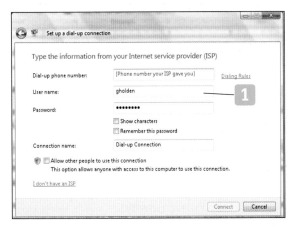

1. Choose a user name that you'll use to log on to the Internet. This can also be used as the account name that you'll use to log on to the Internet and set up your email account. Also choose a memorable password – one that has at least seven characters, a mixture of letters and numbers, and capital and small letters.

2. Provide an email address so you can send and receive email. You'll also need two server names for email: an incoming address (sometimes called a POP3 address) and an outgoing address (called an SMTP address)

3. Create a password that you'll use to secure your Internet connection.

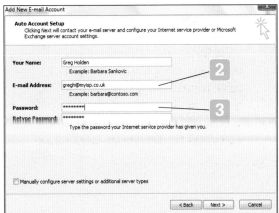

 HOT TIP: Before you sign up with your ISP, find out how you'll receive your cable modem, wireless card, wireless modem or other device. If there's no extra charge it's always nice to have a real, live human being come to your home to set up your connection.

WHAT DOES THIS MEAN?

POP3: Stands for Post Office Protocol, version 3, a system used to deliver incoming messages to the correct email addresses.

SMTP: Stands for Simple Mail Transfer Protocol, a system used to send outgoing email messages.

Connect your computer to the Internet

You'll often see 'free Internet connection' on signs advertising hotels. What they are usually offering is a network technology that transfers data at high speed. The Ethernet is used to convey a high-speed Internet connection from a router to a computer. Here's how to plug your computer into the Ethernet, whether it's at home or during travel.

1 Connect physically to a wired network by plugging your Ethernet cable into the Ethernet port on your computer.

2 When the Set Network Location window appears, select Home, Work or Public (always choose Public at free WiFi hotspots).

3 Click Close.

Set Network Location

Select a location for the 'JolisHomeNetwork' network

This computer is connected to a network. Windows will automatically apply the correct network settings based on the network's location.

Home network
If all the computers on this network are at your home, and you recognize them, this is a trusted home network. Don't choose this for public places such as coffee shops or airports.

Work network
If all the computers on this network are at your workplace, and you recognize them, this is a trusted work network. Don't choose this for public places such as coffee shops or airports.

Public network
If you don't recognize all the computers on the network (for example, you're in a coffee shop or airport, or you have mobile broadband), this is a public network and is not trusted.

☐ Treat all future networks that I connect to as public, and don't ask me again.

Help me choose

Cancel

SEE ALSO: If your computer does not automatically connect to the network, you may need to enable Network Discovery. That process is described in the next task.

HOT TIP: If your computer does not automatically connect to the Internet, go to the System Tray. Click the network connection icon and see if the network you want to connect to is there. If it is, click it and click Connect. If not, you'll need to troubleshoot in the Network and Sharing Center, detailed later.

Check your Internet connection

It's a matter of faith that your computer hooks up to the Internet, right? Some of us need to have visual proof. A Windows utility called Network and Sharing Center is the key to seeing which devices are on your network and how the network is functioning.

1 Click the Network icon on the taskbar and click Open Network and Sharing Center.

2 A working Internet connection is represented like this in the Network and Sharing Center.

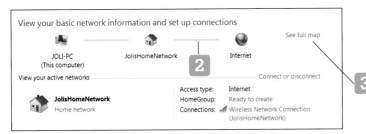

3 Click See full map to view workgroup computers.

4 All computers and devices connected to the network are displayed. You may see a question mark for an unknown device, as shown below.

5 Select the computer you want to use and double-click it to view available items.

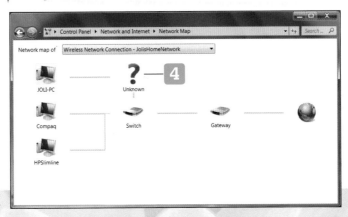

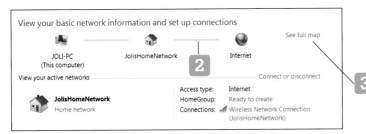

? DID YOU KNOW?

In order to see resources such as folders or printers, you need to have file sharing activated. You also need to have a resource that you have designated as shared.

! ALERT: If you have connected one or more of your computers to the network while they are still on, they may not show up on the network map. You may need to restart them.

Start up Internet Explorer

Internet Explorer is Microsoft's web browser and it is bundled with its Windows operating systems – a fact that has caused the company some legal trouble over the years. Internet Explorer isn't the only web browser around, but it is fully functional and a good tool to use to start surfing the Web.

1 Do one of the following:

- Click the Internet Explorer shortcut icon on your desktop if you have one.

- Click Start and click Internet Explorer.

- Click the Internet Explorer icon just to the right of the Start menu.

2 When the Internet Explorer window opens, type the Web address of the site you want to visit in the Address box.

3 Press Enter to visit the site.

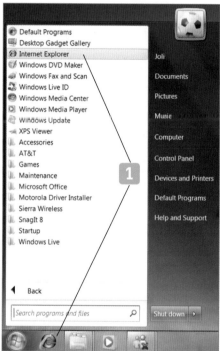

ALERT: Because Internet Explorer is so widely used, hackers regularly contrive to create malicious software that attacks it. Microsoft regularly patches Internet Explorer to combat such attacks, so chances are you won't run into a problem. But you may want to consider installing a free web browser such as Firefox, which is considered more secure.

? DID YOU KNOW?

Once you have visited more than one webpage, the Back and Forward buttons become active. They enable you to revisit previous pages or go forward to subsequent pages respectively.

Navigate to a website

Once you are connected to the Internet, either wirelessly or via a wired Ethernet connection, you can start browsing websites. Windows 7 comes with Microsoft's own web browser, Internet Explorer.

1 Click the Internet Explorer icon just to the right of the Start button on the taskbar (it looks like a blue letter 'e').

2 Click once in the Address bar to highlight the current webpage's address. Or do you say Uniform Resource Locator (URL)?

3 Type a new address and press Enter to go to a new webpage.

SEE ALSO: When Internet Explorer first opens, it displays the default start-up page – probably one configured by your computer manufacturer. You can change this to your own start-up page as described later in this chapter (Change your browser's home page).

Visit multiple websites with browser tabs

You don't have to close one webpage if you want to visit more at the same time. All you have to do is open a website in a new tab. When the new tab opens, just type the address of the next site you want to visit.

1 Open Internet Explorer.

2 Click the New Tab icon. You'll find it if you look to the right of the tab for the current page.

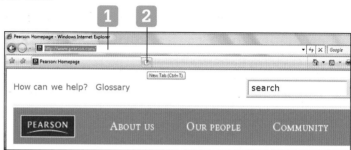

3 When the new tab opens, the address is highlighted. That allows you to quickly type or paste a new one.

4 Press Enter to go to the new page.

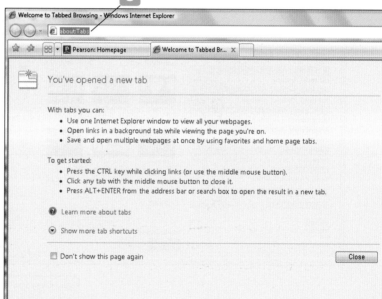

? **DID YOU KNOW?**

Viewing pages in multiple tabs is convenient. It also has the advantage of consuming less computer memory than opening a separate browser window for each webpage.

HOT TIP: Type the following: http://www.microsoft.com

Change your browser's home page

Many people choose a favourite image to be their screen saver. It's also possible to have a favourite page appear when you start up your computer. Maybe it also contains photos of your family or maybe it lets you search the Web (like Google, http://www.google.co.uk). To change your browser's home page, follow these steps.

1 Visit the page that you want to use as your home page.

2 Click the down arrow next to the home icon (it looks like a house).

3 Click Add or Change Home Page.

4 Select one of the options provided (see What Does This Mean? for more explanation).

5 Click Yes.

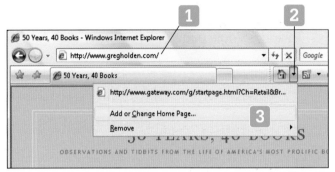

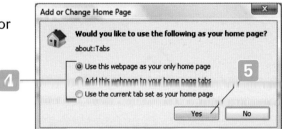

WHAT DOES THIS MEAN?

Use this webpage as your only home page: Choose this if you want only one page to be your home page. (This is the most common option.)

Add this webpage to your home page tabs: Choose this if you want the page to be one of multiple home pages to choose from.

Use the current tab set as your home page: Choose this if you have multiple tabs open in the current browser window and you want them all to function as home pages.

 SEE ALSO: For more on how to navigate to a website, consult 'Navigate to a website' earlier in this chapter.

ALERT: Before you designate a webpage as your home page, take a minute to verify. Make sure you have located the webpage you want and that it is currently displayed in your browser window.

Bookmark a favourite website

If you have a pair of shoes or a jumper that you wear again and again, I'll bet it's at the front of your wardrobe where you can grab it quickly. An online 'favourite' serves much the same purpose: with the help of a bookmark, Internet Explorer returns quickly to a webpage you want to revisit.

1 Navigate to the webpage that's a favourite.

2 Click the Add to Favorites icon. It looks like two stars.

3 To add a single page as a favourite, click Add to Favorites.

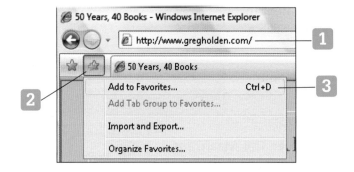

4 Type a name for the website.

5 Click Add.

HOT TIP: Organisation is always a way to make things easier to find. In the next task, you'll learn how to create subfolders within the Favorites folder.

HOT TIP: The option under Add to Favorites, Add Tab Group to Favorites, lets you add all the webpages you currently have open in different tabs to your list of favourites. You add the entire group of tabs together. When you choose this option from the Favorites Center later on, you open all the pages at once.

Change your browser's zoom level

What's a browser anyway? It's what captures such online content as text, images, sounds and video. But maybe you have a strong preference for a particular type face or you would really like the type to be bigger or smaller. Here's how to change your browser's settings.

1 Click Page.

2 When the menu appears, scroll down to Text Size. Note that the directions here are to scroll please don't click this time.

3 When the submenu appears, slide your mouse pointer straight to the left and choose one of the text size options.

4 To enlarge what's on the page, click Page and click Zoom. This will affect everything that's on the page, not just text.

5 Choose a Zoom option. If you're happy with what you see, you're probably looking at the default of 100%.

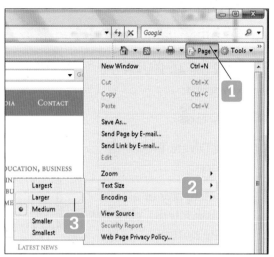

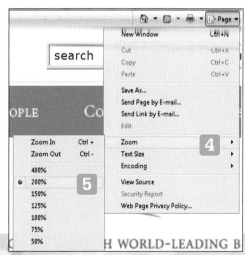

? DID YOU KNOW?

Changing text settings in your browser won't enlarge all the type on the webpage. Text that is formatted as a graphic image won't be affected.

🔥 HOT TIP: Another way to make the contents of your computer monitor appear larger is to change the monitor's resolution.

Clear your browsing history

It used to be that you'd have to hire a private detective if you wanted to find out where someone had gone and what they had done. Now, whether you know it or not, information is being compiled about you all the time through a browsing history that includes a list of websites you've visited and any URLs you've typed. If you don't want others to know your business, you'll need to remove information stored on your computer related to your Internet activities.

1 Open Internet Explorer.

2 Click the Alt key on the keyboard.

3 Click Tools.

4 Click Delete Browsing History.

5 To delete any or all of the listed items, click the Delete button.

6 Click Delete all to erase all stored information at once.

7 Click Close when you've finished.

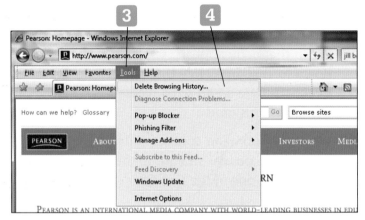

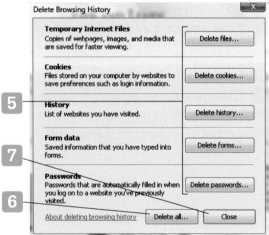

ALERT: Internet Explorer has an autocomplete form data function that allows you to fill out forms automatically. You should delete this option if you don't want others who use your computer to have access to this information.

Stay safe online

There are plenty of books written about online safety. In fact, you'll find my name on several. But just like 'look both ways before you cross the road', a lot of the most important tips are the most obvious.

1. When you are connecting to a network, respond appropriately when prompted by Windows (e.g. Public, Home or Work).

2. Purchase, install and use antivirus software. Don't assume it came with your computer as standard equipment.

3. Stalkers use Facebook and other social networking sites like overeaters use buffet dinners. Think twice before posting confidential information like your home address and personal phone number.

4. If you see an 's' after 'http', you know it's a secure site. Don't make credit card purchases or travel reservations unless the website address starts with https://.

5. Once you sign in to enter a website, always make sure you sign out when you've finished.

> You are logged in as **gholden**| Log Out |

ALERT: After you've finished on a secure site, make sure you sign out. That way the person who uses the computer after you can't use your information and pretend to be you.

? DID YOU KNOW?
Danger doesn't always come in the form of stalkers and identity thieves. Other computer enemies include pets, beverages and cigarette smoke.

Troubleshoot connection problems

Sometimes connections don't work for some reason. Perhaps the signal strength isn't strong enough or Windows needs to refresh its network settings. Well, convenient diagnostic tools to help you troubleshoot the problem are included.

1 Open the Network and Sharing Center.

2 If your Internet connection is not functioning, click the red X.

3 Click the first option to repair the problem.

4 Chances are the problem will be resolved. If not, follow additional steps shown in the Windows Network Diagnostics utility.

5 Click the X in the top right corner of the Network and Sharing Center window to close it.

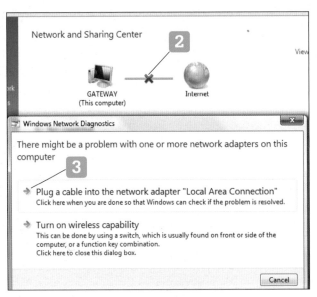

? DID YOU KNOW?

You can also click Troubleshoot problems in the Network and Sharing Center to diagnose and resolve connectivity problems.

HOT TIP: You might see a message instructing you to enable the network adapter. You can do this manually by right-clicking the network connection icon and choosing Enable from the context menu.

9 Email, Skype and social networking

Introduction

Just like the old song says, the goal is to make new friends while keeping the old (the one is silver and the other is gold). In this chapter, you'll become proficient at Windows Live Mail, Skype and other Internet technologies to communicate instantly with both new and old acquaintances.

Windows Live Mail makes it easy for you to view email, send messages, manage your contacts and print and store your electronic correspondence. To use Windows Live Mail, you need an email address and two email server addresses, which you obtain from your ISP. In fact, you probably already gathered that information while working on Chapter 8. With this information at hand, you can set up email when prompted by the Windows Live Mail wizard. In no time, you'll be online, sending and receiving your own email.

Obtain Windows Live Mail

Windows 7 does not come with an email program; you have to obtain one yourself. Windows Live Mail is free and is the closest thing available to the older email programs you're already used to. Although there are other options, I think Windows Live Mail is the best.

1 With your web browser, visit http://download.live.com.

2 Click Download. You'll be prompted to choose the programs you want to install. At the very least, install Windows Live Mail, Live Toolbar, Live Photo Gallery and Live Messenger.

3 Wait while the download and installation process completes.

4 When prompted to get a Live ID, do so.

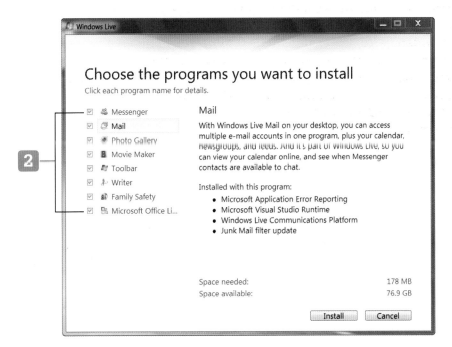

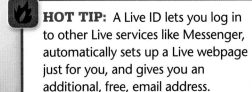 **HOT TIP:** Windows Live Mail integrates seamlessly with other 'Live' applications, like the Toolbar and Photo Gallery.

HOT TIP: A Live ID lets you log in to other Live services like Messenger, automatically sets up a Live webpage just for you, and gives you an additional, free, email address.

Getting started with Windows Live Mail

Just as there's a process and procedure for sending snail mail, there's a way to send and receive email. Actually email is even easier because you get prompts on how to gather information about your email address and mail servers the first time you open Windows Live Mail.

1 Click Start and in the Start Search Window, type Mail. Click Windows Live Mail.

2 If a wizard does not start automatically, click Add e-mail account.

> **HOT TIP:** You can add multiple email accounts by performing these steps again, for each account desired.

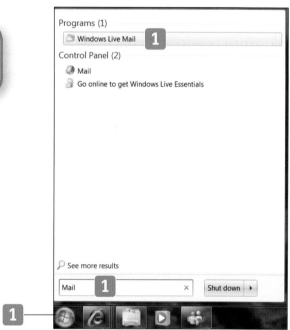

WHAT DOES THIS MEAN?

Display name: When you send an email message, this is the name that appears in the From line. Put your real name and address here rather than your email address.

User name and passcards: When you connect to your ISP's website to pay bills or change other account information, you use a user name. The password keeps your email and account information private. Usually passwords are case-sensitive.

Email address: When you obtained Internet access from an Internet Service Provider you received a default email address. If your user name is rkipling and your provider's URL ends with provider.co.uk, chances are your email address is rkipling@ provider.co.uk. But be sure to verify your user name with your ISP.

3 Type your email address and password.

4 Type your display name.

5 Leave Manually configure server settings for e-mail account unticked. Click Next.

6 If prompted, fill in the information for your incoming and outgoing mail servers. Click Next.

7 If desired, click Set this account as the default mail account in the final wizard screen.

8 Click Finish.

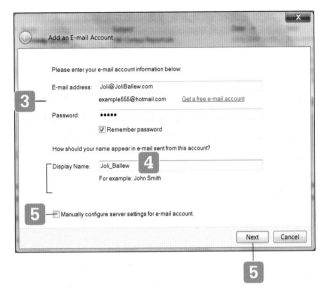

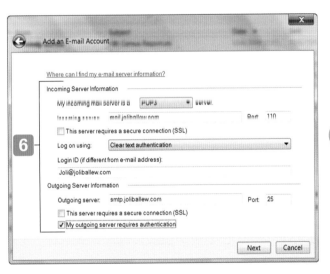

? DID YOU KNOW?

Here's something else you need to obtain from your Internet service provider: an email address and the name of the servers that will route your outgoing and incoming mail.

HOT TIP: In case you don't want to use Windows Live Mail, or if you just want an alternative email service, you can obtain free email from Google (with its Gmail service) or Yahoo! (with Yahoo! Mail).

HOT TIP: Make sure, when you enter your password, that you tick the box telling Windows Live Mail to remember it, so you don't have to enter it each time you check for new mail.

Read your email

There's nothing more depressing than a mailbox with cobwebs, so Windows Live Mail provides you with your first welcome message. To see if others have arrived, click the Sync button. By default Windows Live Mail will check for new messages automatically every 30 minutes.

1 Click Sync button.

2 Click any email once to select it.

3 View the contents of the email.

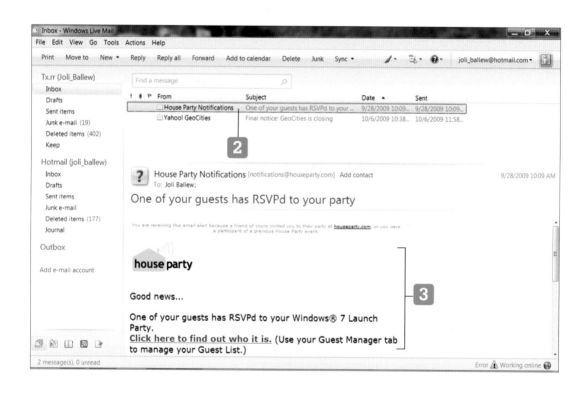

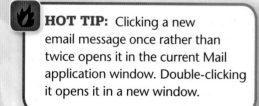

HOT TIP: Clicking a new email message once rather than twice opens it in the current Mail application window. Double-clicking it opens it in a new window.

ALERT: Email is received in the Inbox. If Inbox is not selected, do that first.

ALERT: Click the yellow bar if the email contains images that are not being displayed.

Open an attachment

An attachment can be a picture, document or video clip. Here's what to do when you see a paperclip to find out what's inside. Then enjoy!

1 Click the email once in the Message pane.

2 Double-click the attachment in the Preview pane.

3 If you trust the sender and know what the attachment is, click Open. Otherwise, click Cancel.

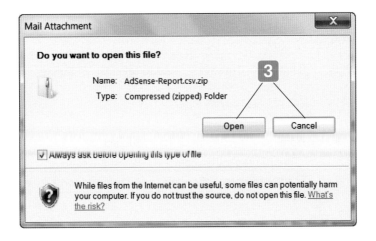

> **ALERT:** Not all attachments are happy surprises. Hackers frequently send messages with attachments that contain malicious code such as viruses. Be very careful when opening attachments from someone you don't know, even if they look interesting and legitimate. Be especially wary if the user's name ends in .zip.

Respond to an email message

Going back and forth between sender and receiver is what happens to most emails. Follow the steps below to reply to someone who has sent an email to you.

1 Select the email you want to reply to in the Message pane.

2 Click Reply.

3 Make sure the email address is accurate.

4 Change the subject line in the Subject field if you wish.

5 Type the message in the body pane.

6 Click Send.

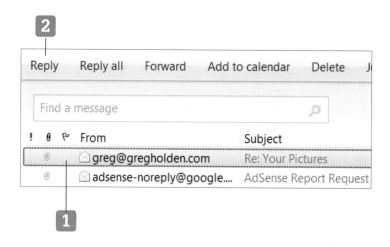

 HOT TIP: Type an email address in the Cc field if you want to copy someone on your message. To send your email to multiple recipients, separate each by a semicolon. When you are responding to a message, the To address has a semicolon pre-entered at the end.

 ALERT: If you're not the only one who received the email, you'll send your response to all of them if you click Reply all. If you want only the sender to read your response, click Reply.

Compose and send a message

When you're the one who starts the conversation, you'll need to compose and send a brand new email. The steps are nearly the same as replying to one you've received.

1 Click New. `New ▾`

2 In the To field, type the email address of the recipient.

3 Type a subject in the Subject field.

4 Type the message in the body pane.

5 Click Send.

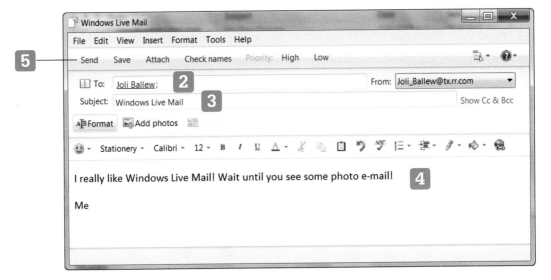

HOT TIP: The formatting controls just above the message composition area let you format parts of your message in bold or italic for emphasis.

? DID YOU KNOW?
The menu bar at the top of the message composition window lets you cut, paste and spell check a message's contents. The tools let you copy text from a word-processing file, for instance.

HOT TIP: Make sure your subject is clear and specific so recipients know what the email is about if they want to open it later.

Insert an image into the message body

When you attach a file, it is sent along with the text of your message but it is separate. It is up to the recipient to open the image. Windows Live Mail also lets you insert an image directly into the body of the message. That way it appears instantly the moment the recipient starts to read your text.

1 Click New.

2 Type the email address of the recipient.

3 Type a subject line.

4 Type your message and press Enter twice to provide some space.

5 Click Add photos.

6 Select the photos to add and click Done when finished.

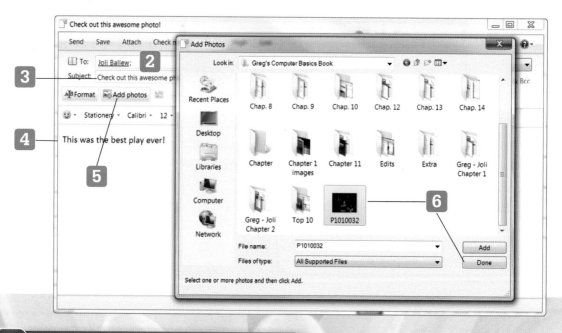

HOT TIP: If the image you have added is too big or you want to delete it, click it once and then press the Delete or Backspace key.

7 The image will appear inside the email body.

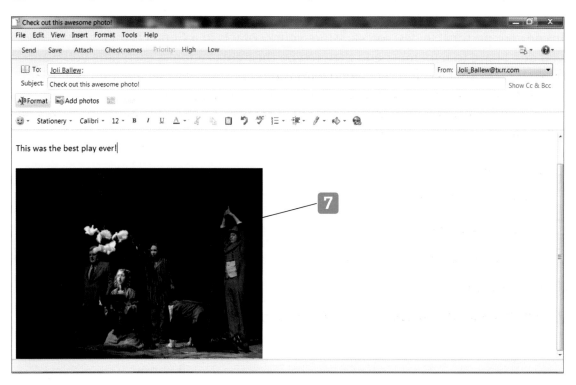

7

ALERT: The same size rules that apply to attaching image files apply to inserting them into message text. But in this case, the bigger the image, the harder it will be for someone to see it in its entirety. Only insert images that are small in size – perhaps 200K to 300K. It's better to attach those that are larger.

Add someone as a contact

Inside your personal folder, you can store your contacts in a Contacts folder. That way, you don't have to remember and then retype their email address each time you want to send them a message. That not only saves time but prevents emails from bouncing back because of typos.

1 From Windows Live Mail, click the Contacts icon. You'll find it in the bottom left corner.

2 Click File.

3 Click Add a contact.

4 Type all of the information you want to add. Be sure to add information to each tab.

5 Click Add contact when you're finished.

6 Click the red X in the Contacts window to close it.

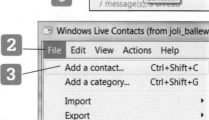

🔥 **HOT TIP:** After you receive a message from a person, right-click their name in your Inbox. Choose Add sender to contacts from the context menu. Their correct name and email address are added instantly.

? **DID YOU KNOW?**
Once you add someone to your Contacts list, you click the Contacts icon and then double-click their name in your list of contacts.

Clean out your old email

Everything needs to be tidied up from time to time. It's especially important to clean out your old email if you don't need it. It saves disk space and makes old messages easier to find when you need them. Here's how to send an individual message to the trash and then empty the trash.

1. Right-click the email message.

2. Click Delete to send the message to Deleted items. (You can also click Delete on the toolbar.)

3. Right-click Deleted items.

4. Click Empty 'Deleted items' folder.

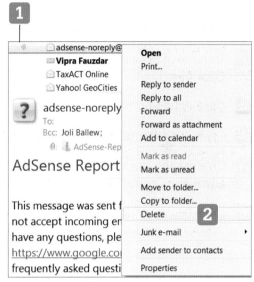

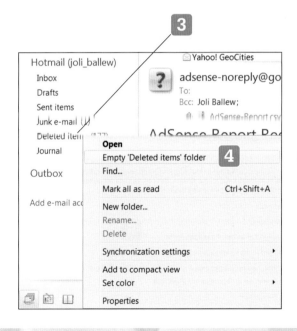

 ALERT: Cleaning out your trash is especially important if your ISP sets a limit on the amount of storage space you can use for email. The more email sitting in your Inbox and other folders, the more memory you consume. If you go over your limit, you won't be able to send or receive email until you clean out old messages and free up more memory.

ALERT: Something else you need to clean out from time to time is your Sent Items folder. Every time you send a message, a copy sits in this folder until you delete it.

Check for new email messages

Windows Live Mail, like other mail programs, will automatically connect to your ISP's email server periodically and retrieve any new messages you have. But if you're the impatient type, you can manually check for mail at any time. You can also change how often Mail looks for email.

1 To check for email manually, click the Sync button.

2 To control how often Mail checks for email, click Tools.

3 Click Options.

4 Click the General tab.

5 Change the number of minutes from 30 to a different number.

6 Click OK.

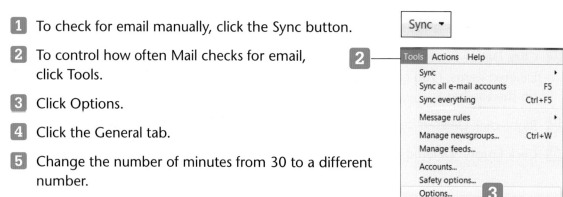

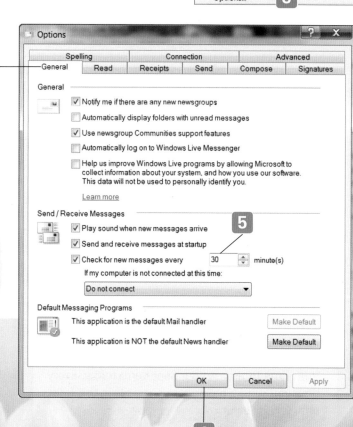

ALERT: You need to be connected to the Internet to check for your email.

? DID YOU KNOW?
You can change other settings in Mail from the other tabs in the Options dialogue box.

Print email

You will want to save some messages offline. Windows Live Mail gives you the chance to do this by either printing the mail message itself or an attachment. After clicking the Print command, the Print dialogue box appears so you can select a printer, the range of pages you want, the number of copies and other options.

1 Select the email you want to print.

2 Click File and click Print.

3 Choose the printer you want to use.

4 Click the up or down arrows to adjust the number of copies.

5 Click here and type the number of pages, if necessary.

6 Click Print.

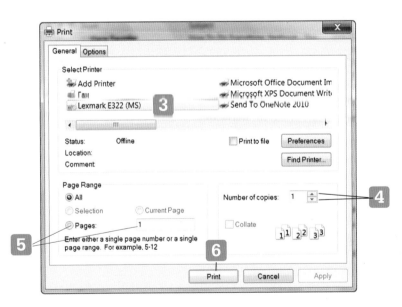

? DID YOU KNOW?

You can configure print preferences by clicking Preferences in the Print dialogue box. Preferences depend on the printer, but typically include print quality and black-and-white versus colour.

HOT TIP: Another way to open the Print dialogue box is to press Ctrl+P.

File your email in a folder

It takes some effort to create a folder in the first place and a little bit more effort to use it. But having an organised Inbox is worth the trouble of moving email from one folder to another. You can drag and drop email you want to move, or you can use the Move to button on the toolbar.

1 Click the email message that you want to move in the Message pane.

2 Click Move to on the toolbar.

3 Click the folder to move the item to, and click OK.

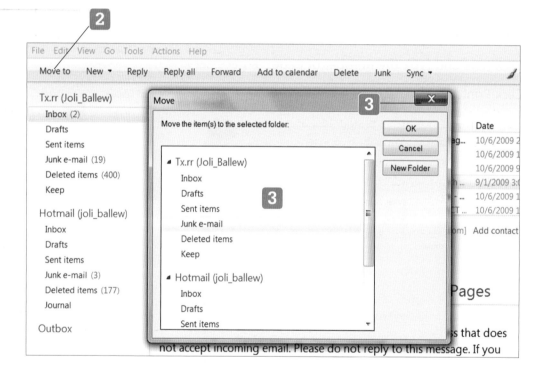

HOT TIP: You can move multiple messages at the same time by selecting and moving them at once. To select a group of contiguous messages, click the first one in the group, press the Shift key and click the last one in the group. To select a group of discontiguous messages, click the first one, press the Ctrl key and click each one in turn.

HOT TIP: Create your own folders by right-clicking Inbox and selecting New folder.

Create your own email signature

Just like you have a return address on the upper left-hand corner of your snail mail envelope, you can create a signature to appear at the bottom of your emails. This is even better, because you can add more of your particulars and even a point to ponder.

1 Open the Options dialogue box by choosing Tools > Options in Windows Live Mail.

2 Click the Signatures tab.

3 Click New.

4 Type the text for your signature, pressing Enter after each line.

5 Select the Add signatures to all outgoing messages tick box. Make sure that the signature is selected as the default. Or, if you want to add your signature only occasionally, select the Don't add signatures to Replies and Forwards tick box.

6 Click OK to save the signature.

HOT TIP: If you have different email accounts and want to assign a different signature to each one, go to the Signatures tab of the Options dialogue box. There, select a signature in the Signatures list box, click the Advanced button, then select an account to associate it with.

ALERT: If you use some emails for professional purposes, review the contact information before you include it. Also make sure that any quote or pithy comment you want to include is appropriate.

Make a phone call with your computer

Voice over Internet Protocol (VoIP) is a technology that you can use to make calls to anywhere in the world from your computer. What's more, a webcam can add video to create a video phone system. One of the most popular such services is called Skype (www.skype.com).

1 Visit the Skype home page and download the software for your computer.

2 Make a test call using a microphone you connect to your computer.

3 Enter a list of contacts such as you have for instant messaging or email.

4 Choose a contact and click a button either to call another computer that is equipped with VoIP or call a regular handheld or mobile phone.

5 If you plan to call landline or mobile phones, you'll have to deposit money with Skype beforehand, which the service holds for you on credit.

DID YOU KNOW?

If you use Skype to make a call from your computer to a landline phone or mobile phone, you are charged a basic fee, which is much less than traditional long distance. Often there is only a nominal charge for international calls. If you use your computer to call someone else's computer using Skype, there is no charge at all.

HOT TIP: You can also make calls on your computer using a VoIP phone service such as VoIPTalk or VoIP Internet Phone (www.voipfone.co.uk). If you don't want to be disturbed while working on your computer, you can block calls temporarily. Many VoIP services offer features such as voicemail, caller ID and call forwarding.

Participate on Facebook

Facebook is one of the most popular forums for keeping up with family and friends, and it's not just for young people either. Many over-50s (including the author) check into Facebook regularly to see what's up with family and friends and to view photos of their children and their families.

1 Go to the Facebook home page for the UK (http://en-gb.facebook.com).

2 Fill out your contact information on the site's home page.

3 Click the green Sign Up button.

4 Fill out your personal information.

5 Click Photos to add your photo to your profile.

6 Search for acquaintances by name or email address and invite them to become 'friends'.

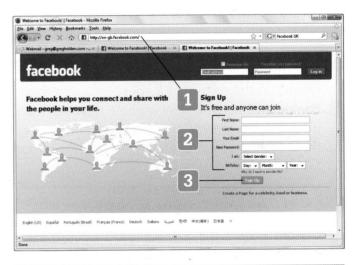

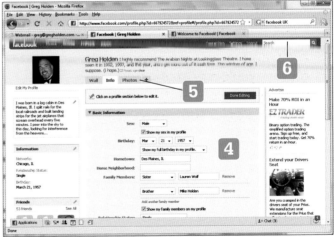

HOT TIP: Before you sign up, get a relative or friend to take a photo of you with a digital camera and save the file on your computer so you can add it to your Facebook profile.

ALERT: Postings on Facebook or another discussion board can stay up for years, which gives you time to review comments and think about how to respond. Unless you save a copy of a chat, the text will be gone because it's an online space where people talk back and forth in real time via text.

Create a blog

The term 'blog' comes from the phrase 'Web log', which pretty much says it all. Unlike the diary that you locked and hid under your mattress, you're inviting others to share their ideas on your thoughts.

1 Create a blog space. You can usually use your email or you can go to a blog space service such as www.blogger.com. In any case, it's often free and simple to sign up.

2 Choose your settings after deciding whether to allow public access or to allow only those you know to participate.

3 Decide whether you want a photo of yourself on your blog and determine other blog design elements. In addition to choosing colours and fonts, you can decide the design of postings, archives of older postings and responses.

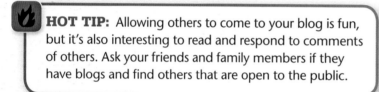

HOT TIP: Allowing others to come to your blog is fun, but it's also interesting to read and respond to comments of others. Ask your friends and family members if they have blogs and find others that are open to the public.

10 Work with digital photos

Introduction

Taking, editing and storing your photos is magic once you know how. Following the steps in this chapter will allow you to spend more time enjoying and less time fussing over them. Unfortunately, you won't find a photo-editing program in Windows 7. As with email, you'll have to get a program on your own.

Get Windows Live Photo Gallery

In the last chapter you learned how to get Windows Live Mail. During that task, I suggested you also get Windows Live Photo Gallery, Live Messenger and Live Toolbar. If you did that, great, you can skip this task. If you didn't, here are the steps again.

1 With your web browser, visit http://download.live.com.

2 Click Download. You'll be prompted to choose the programs you want to install. At the very least, install Windows Live Mail, Live Toolbar, Live Photo Gallery and Live Messenger.

3 Wait while the download and installation process completes.

4 When prompted to get a Live ID, do so.

HOT TIP: A Live ID lets you log into other Live services like Messenger, automatically sets up a Live Web page just for you, and gives you an additional, free, email address.

HOT TIP: Windows Live Photo Gallery integrates with your Windows Live Mail contacts, Live Messenger contacts and the Live Toolbar to make it easier than ever to post photos on the Web.

Import an image from your digital camera

Anything on your digital camera can be stored in your computer. Here's how to get images from there to here.

1 Turn on your digital camera.

2 Connect the camera to one of your computer's USB ports.

3 Click Import pictures and videos using Windows Live Photo Gallery.

4 Click Import all new items now.

5 Type a name for the group of photos to import.

6 Click Import.

🔥 **HOT TIP:** The AutoPlay dialogue box automatically appears when you connect your digital camera and Windows detects it. Choose View pictures if you don't want to use the wizard and prefer browsing and copying photos with Windows Explorer.

❓ **DID YOU KNOW?**
You'll get the same prompts if you insert a media card into a card slot. This may be more convenient if you have the appropriate hardware.

View images with Window Live Photo Gallery

You can view images in Windows Live Photo Gallery simply by opening the program. The navigation options are very similar to the Windows Explorer windows you've seen before. However, in Live Photo Gallery you have other options, like View Slideshow, E-mail, Print and more. Here's how to view digital photos.

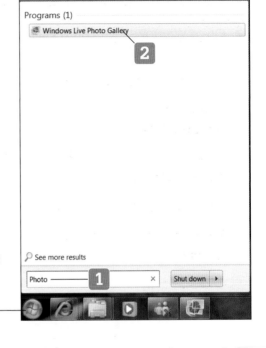

1 Click Start, and in the Start Search window type Photo.

2 In the results, click Windows Live Photo Gallery.

3 Browse the folders in the left pane to locate the images you want. You can also click All photos and videos.

4 Click the Slide show button to view the photos as a slide show, if desired.

5 Click Esc on the keyboard to stop the slide show.

 **HOT TIP:** By default, your pictures are stored in the Pictures folder, not by or 'in' Photo Gallery.

HOT TIP: Double-click any photo to edit it. Just click Fix and the editing options will appear.

Automatically edit a photo

You'll have photos to edit, including those with red-eye, those that need cropping and those that are too light or too dark. Here's how to view what you want, not what exists in reality, using Windows Live Photo Gallery.

1 Open Windows Live Photo Gallery and double-click any picture that needs editing.

2 Click the controls at the bottom of the Photo Gallery window to rotate the image, if necessary.

3 Click on the Fix button to access the editing tools you need.

4 Adjust the individual controls that appear. (You can always click Undo if you don't like something.)

5 The edited image is displayed in Windows Live Photo Gallery.

6 Click Back to gallery to save the changes.

ALERT: If you want to keep the original photo, make a copy before you start to edit. Don't forget to save your changes.

HOT TIP: The Auto Adjust option lets Windows Live Photo Gallery do the work of editing for you, based on the content of the photo.

Crop a photo

Most of the time, the images you take with your digital camera will contain material you don't need. The process of deleting the parts of an image that aren't needed so that only the most important contents remain is known as cropping.

1 Open the image you want to crop by double-clicking it.

2 When the image opens in Windows Live Photo Gallery, click Fix.

3 Click Crop photo.

4 Adjust the selection rectangle so it encloses the part of the image you want to preserve.

5 Click Apply.

? **DID YOU KNOW?**

Cropping an image can dramatically reduce its file size. This makes it easier to store, email and publish on the Web.

? **DID YOU KNOW?**

Cropping calls attention to the people or objects in an image that you want viewers to focus on primarily.

Adjust brightness and contrast

Remember when you had to twiddle with dials on your television until you got the picture quality just right? Now you can do the same thing on your computer to improve the visual quality of your photos.

1 Open Windows Live Photo Gallery.

2 Double-click a picture to edit.

3 Click Fix.

4 Click Auto adjust to get Live Photo Gallery to make some initial changes.

5 Click Adjust exposure.

6 Move the sliders for Brightness and Contrast.

7 Click Back to gallery to save your changes.

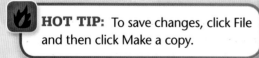

HOT TIP: To save changes, click File and then click Make a copy.

HOT TIP: To open Windows Live Photo Gallery, click Start, type Photo Gallery in the Start Search window and when Windows Live Photo Gallery appears in the Start menu, click it.

? DID YOU KNOW?
If you don't like the result at any time, just click Undo.

Adjust the colour quality of an image

Even if you're colour blind, the computer makes it easy to get the colour just right.

1 Open Windows Live Photo Gallery.

2 Double-click a picture to edit.

3 Click Fix.

4 Click Auto adjust if you want Live Photo Gallery to make initial changes.

5 Click Adjust color.

6 Move the sliders for Color temperature, Tint and Saturation.

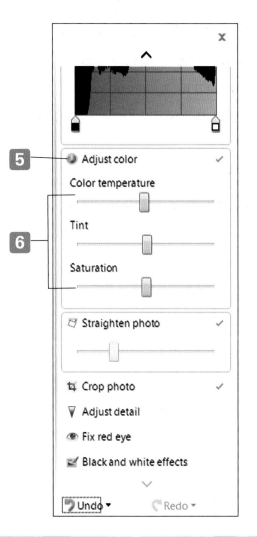

? DID YOU KNOW?
If you're not happy with what you see, click Undo to return to the original image settings.

🔥 HOT TIP: Mood varies with settings. Temperature runs from blue to yellow, tint runs from green to red, and saturation moves from black and white to colour.

Copy images from a media card

Instead of connecting a digital camera directly to your computer, another option is to copy images from a USB flash drive or a small portable memory device called an SD card. Your digital camera's memory card can also be removed and inserted into a USB card reader you purchase and then connect to your computer. Many card readers can accommodate all of the digital camera memory cards you can buy.

1 Connect the media card to your computer. Usually, this requires you to insert the card into an appropriate slot.

2 The AutoPlay window will open automatically.

3 Click on the Import pictures and videos using Windows Live Photo Gallery option.

4 Click Import all new items now, and type a name for the group of images.

5 Click Import.

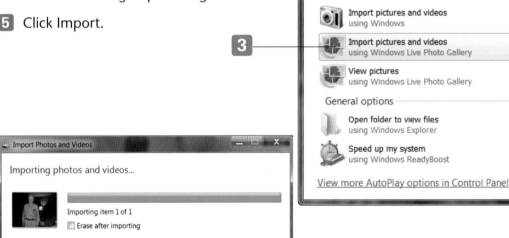

? **DID YOU KNOW?**

Tick the Erase after importing box to have the images automatically erased from your media card after the pictures have been imported.

? **DID YOU KNOW?**

After they have been downloaded, photos will be displayed in Windows Live Photo Gallery.

Play a slide show

If you ever want to show your family or friends a set of related photos in sequence, you no longer have to mount a series of slides in a projector. As you already know, you can view a slide show in Windows Live Photo Gallery. You can also offer a slide show in any Explorer window.

1 Click start and click Pictures.

2 Open any folder that contains pictures you want to view in a slide show.

3 Click Slide show.

4 Click Esc to stop the slide show.

? DID YOU KNOW?

You can choose pictures in a folder to serve as a screen saver. Open the Personalization window in Control Panel, and from the screen saver options, browse to the folder to use.

Add a tag to a photo

If you have a dog named Muffy, you can attach the tag 'Muffy' to all the photos you take of him so you can display them altogether or even create a slide show of them.

1 Open Windows Live Photo Gallery.

2 Click Descriptive tags.

3 Click Add new tab.

4 Type a tag name and then click anywhere outside it.

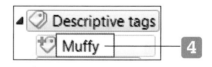

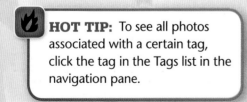

HOT TIP: To see all photos associated with a certain tag, click the tag in the Tags list in the navigation pane.

5 Select pictures to which the tag should be applied.

6 Drag those files to the tag name under Descriptive tags.

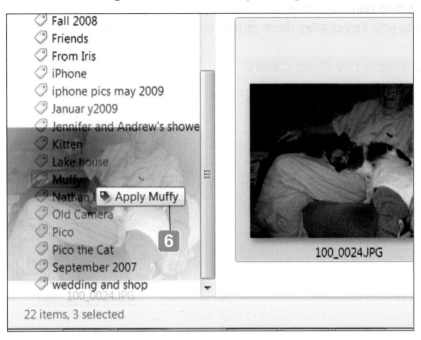

Fall 2008
Friends
From Iris
iPhone
iphone pics may 2009
Januar y2009
Jennifer and Andrew's showe
Kitten
Lake house
Muffy
Nathan ▸ Apply Muffy
Old Camera
Pico
Pico the Cat
September 2007
wedding and shop
100_0024.JPG

6

100_0024.JPG

22 items, 3 selected

7 Alternatively, right-click the image and choose Properties. Check the Details tab is selected and type the tag name as shown here.

100_0025 Properties

General | Security | **Details** | Previous Versions

Property	Value
Description	
Title	
Subject	
Rating	☆ ☆ ☆ ☆ ☆
Tags	Muffy:
Comments	
Origin	
Authors	
Date taken	8/17/2006 3:43 PM
Program name	Version 1.0700
Date acquired	
Copyright	
Image	
Image ID	
Dimensions	2304 x 1728
Width	2304 pixels
Height	1728 pixels
Horizontal resolution	230 dpi
Vertical resolution	230 dpi

7

Remove Properties and Personal Information

OK | Cancel | Apply

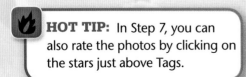

HOT TIP: In Step 7, you can also rate the photos by clicking on the stars just above Tags.

Arrange photos by date

You can view the photos by their dates taken by selecting the proper year from the navigation pane in Windows Live Photo Gallery.

1 Open Windows Live Photo Gallery.

2 Click a date in the Date taken section of the pane on the left.

3 To change the entry for the date taken of any photo, right-click the photo and choose Properties. Check the Details tab is selected and from the resulting dialogue box, type the desired date.

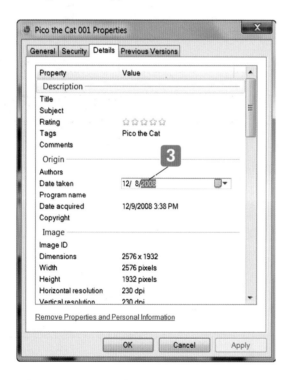

 HOT TIP: Collapse groups for tags and folders; expand the group for Date taken.

 HOT TIP: You can also click the calendar icon and choose a new date from the pop-up calendar.

Burn photos to a CD or DVD

It's great to have a backup or to be able to snail mail or hand deliver copies of those lovely holiday photos. It's also nice to create a DVD for someone who does not have a computer!

1. Insert a writable CD or DVD into your disk drive.

2. Open Windows Live Photo Gallery.

3. Select the photos to burn to a DVD.

4. Click the Make button at the top of the Photo Gallery window.

5. Choose Burn a DVD.

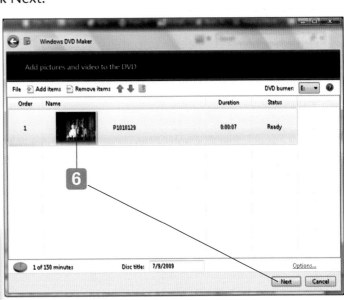

6. In the resulting Windows DVD Maker dialogue box, click the image and then click Next.

7. In the resulting Ready to Burn Disc window, click the Burn button.

8. When a confirming dialogue box appears and your disk drawer opens, click Finish to complete the process and close the wizard.

 HOT TIP: Select all is an option from the File menu, should you want to burn all your photos to a DVD.

 HOT TIP: Hold down the Ctrl key while clicking the images to select additional images.

? DID YOU KNOW?
You can modify the disk title or adjust the recording speed before clicking Next to activate the progress bar.

Explore additional sharing options

There are many more ways to share your pictures in Windows Live Photo Gallery, but not enough room to detail them all here. However, you should explore them. Here are some options to try:

1 File > Screen saver settings – to configure a screen saver with your favourite photos. Click this to open the Screen Saver dialogue box.

2 Publish > Online album – to send selected photos to your Windows Live webpage. If you signed up for a Windows Live ID as prompted in Chapter 9, your Live webpage is ready for you to upload photos today.

3 Publish > More services – to publish on Flickr, or to add plug-ins for other social networking websites, like Facebook, YouTube and Multiply.

HOT TIP: If you don't have a Live ID, go to http://idsignup.live.com.

4 Make > Create
   panoramic photo
   – to stitch together
   multiple, similar
   photos to create a
   single, panoramic
   photo.

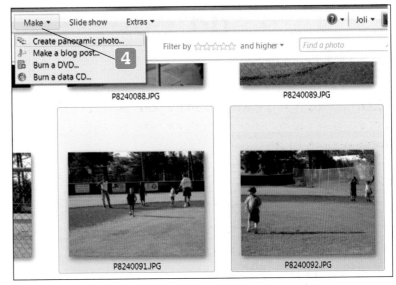

5 Make > Make a blog
   post – to create
   a blog post with
   Windows Live Writer,
   a Windows Live free
   application.

6 Make > Burn a data
   CD – to burn a CD with the selected pictures. CDs created in this manner can be
   played on most computers.

7 And finally, E-mail and Print! Click E-mail to automatically insert pictures into an
   email, as shown here.

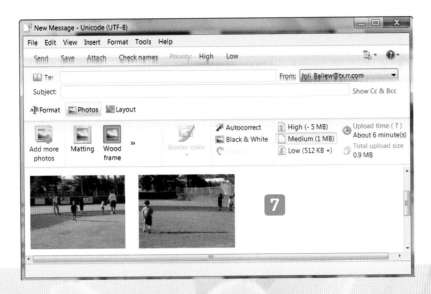

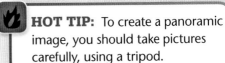

HOT TIP: To create a panoramic
image, you should take pictures
carefully, using a tripod.

11 Manage audio and video

Introduction

By this time it should be clear that computers can do much more than simple computing. Your new electronic device can get you online, where you can exchange messages with friends and family and keep up with current events and it can be a creative outlet as well. You can organise and play audio and video files, entertain yourself and indulge your creative side, too.

In this chapter, I have collected tasks that describe some common ways you can use your new computer to play and work with audio and video files. You'll learn how to use your computer as a source of entertainment to bring you music, television and Internet radio as well.

Get started with Windows Media Player

When I use the word 'media' here, I'm talking about digital content such as music or videos. Media Player is one of the applications that can play music and movies, and it's one you may already be familiar with from previous versions of Windows. By default, Media Player is configured to play music. But once you know where the right controls are, you can play other media as well.

1 Click the Media Player icon on the taskbar.

2 Locate the Library button.

3 Click the arrow next to Library to select a category.

4 Click Music to play a music file.

? **DID YOU KNOW?**

Windows Media Player can be used to copy music onto blank CDs. Insert a blank CD into your computer's CD/ DVD writer. Select songs, albums or playlists you want to burn. Select Burn to copy the songs to the CD.

HOT TIP: The Windows Media Player can also be used to organise your music and videos by creating your own playlists.

! ALERT: The first time you open Media Player version 12, you'll be asked to set up the program. Choose the recommended settings.

Manage your digital music

Once you have Windows Media Player open, you'll find it easy to open any music track. You'll discover, in fact, that several music selections are provided for you along with Windows. Songs are listed in the navigation pane.

1 Open Media Player.

2 In the left navigation pane, click Music.

3 To play a song or album, double-click it.

If you have music stored on other PCs on a network:

4 Click Organize, Manage libraries and Music.

5 Click Add and browse to the folder to add.

6 Click Include folder.

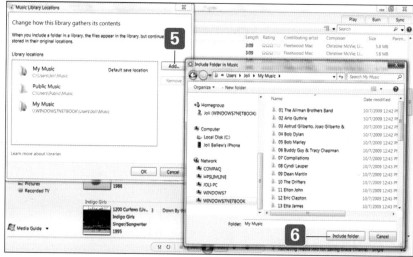

Play a CD

Playing a CD on your computer is easy. You have several options for playing a file – all you have to do is insert the CD in your computer's disk drive and then choose the option you want.

1 Insert a music CD in your computer's CD-ROM drive.

2 When Windows Media Player opens, it should begin to play the CD automatically. If it does not, click the Pause/Play button.

3 Click one of the track numbers to move to another track on the CD.

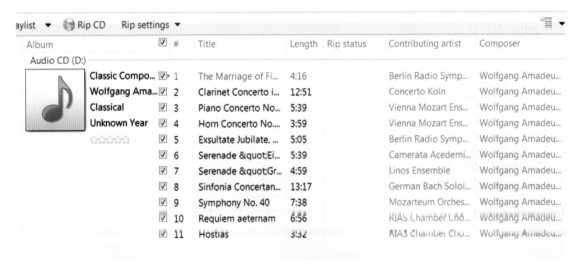

4 At the bottom of the interface are navigational controls, as shown here.

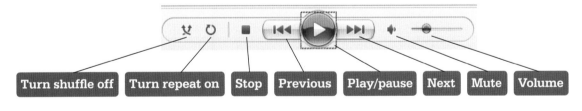

Turn shuffle off | Turn repeat on | Stop | Previous | Play/pause | Next | Mute | Volume

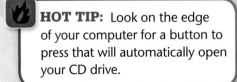 **HOT TIP:** Look on the edge of your computer for a button to press that will automatically open your CD drive.

! ALERT: To close your CD drive, you can gently push the drive and it will retract by itself into your computer. But if you push too hard, you might damage the drive. It's safer to press the same button you used to open the drive to close it as well.

Assemble a playlist

A set of audio files that have been grouped together and are intended to be played in sequence is called a playlist. Playlists are especially useful if you want background music to play at home while you are cooking or entertaining, or in the car while you're driving. Windows Media Player makes it easy for you to assemble a playlist.

1 Click the icon for Windows Media Player on the taskbar.

2 Click Playlists.

3 If no playlists have been created, you'll see the option Click here. Click it.

4 Type a name for your playlist in the text box that appears in the left-hand pane. Click anywhere outside the text box to finish entering the name.

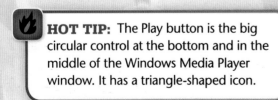

HOT TIP: The Play button is the big circular control at the bottom and in the middle of the Windows Media Player window. It has a triangle-shaped icon.

5 Click one of the items under Library in the left-hand column.

6 Drag an item from the centre of the Media Player window to the playlist on the right.

7 Repeat step 6 until the playlist has been assembled.

8 Note the new Play options on the right side of Media Player. You can save the list, clear the list or reorder the list items by dragging and dropping.

9 Click Save list.

Turn up the volume

Once you start playing audio files, you'll naturally want to make sure you can hear what you want to play. You've got a couple of options when it comes to adjusting the volume.

1 First, click the volume icon in the System Tray.

2 Move the slider up to increase the volume, down to decrease it.

3 Move the volume slider on the Windows Media Player window to the right to increase volume, to the left to decrease it.

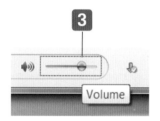

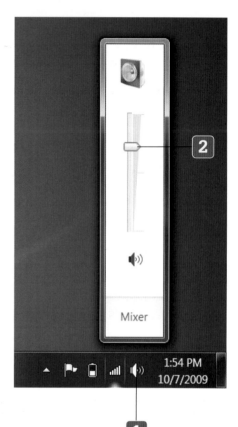

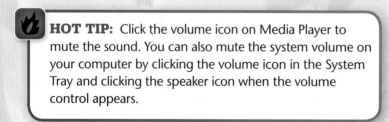

? DID YOU KNOW?

On some computers, pressing Fn (Function) and then clicking PgUp will increase volume and holding down Fn while clicking PgDn will decrease volume.

🔥 HOT TIP: Click the volume icon on Media Player to mute the sound. You can also mute the system volume on your computer by clicking the volume icon in the System Tray and clicking the speaker icon when the volume control appears.

Configure external speakers

Computers aren't created for high fidelity audio. Most built-in computer speakers are not high quality. By configuring external speakers you can dramatically improve the volume and quality of the sound you play.

1 Purchase some external speakers and connect them to your computer at the appropriate port (usually marked with a small speaker icon). If necessary, turn them on.

2 Click Start and in the Start Search window type Manage Audio Devices. Click it in the results.

3 When the Sound dialogue box opens, double-click Speakers.

4 Click the Levels tab.

HOT TIP: If you see a small red x on the speaker icon shown on the Levels tab, click it to activate the speakers.

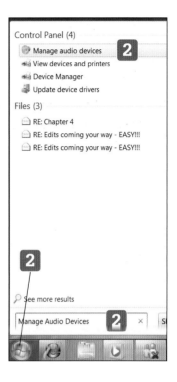

Control Panel (4)

- Manage audio devices **2**
- View devices and printers
- Device Manager
- Update device drivers

Files (3)

- RE: Chapter 4
- RE: Edits coming your way - EASY!!!
- RE: Edits coming your way - EASY!!!

See more results

Manage Audio Devices **2**

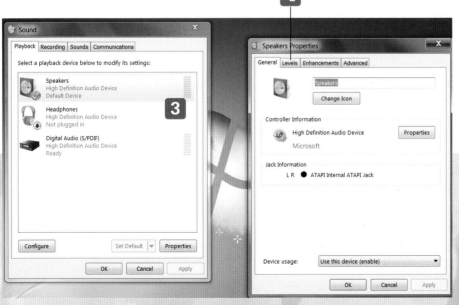

5 Move the slider to adjust the speaker volume.

6 Click Balance.

7 When the Balance dialogue box opens, move the L (Left) and R (Right) sliders to change the sound balance.

8 Click OK here and twice more to close all open dialogue boxes and preserve your new settings.

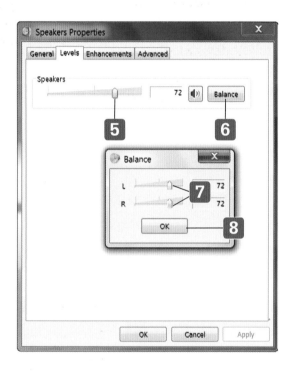

? **DID YOU KNOW?**

You can test your speakers by clicking the Advanced tab of the Speakers Properties dialogue box. Choose your speaker configuration and click the Test button.

Copy a CD to your hard drive

If you have a favourite music CD, you can copy it to your computer's hard disk. When you have the audio files on disk, you can then copy them to a portable music player or other device.

1 Load the CD into your computer's disk drive.

2 If any pop-up boxes appear, click the X to close them.

3 When the CD loads in Windows Media Player, it will begin to play. Click the Stop button if desired.

4 Deselect any songs you do not want to copy.

5 Click Rip CD.

? DID YOU KNOW?
By default, audio files you copy are saved in the Music folder.

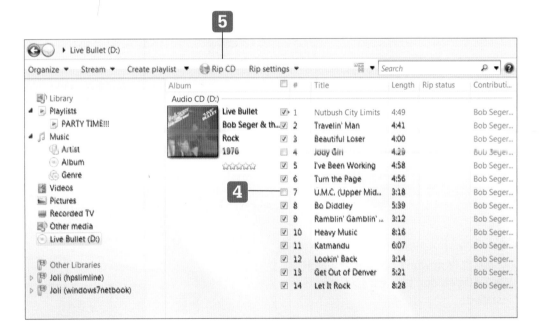

? DID YOU KNOW?
The term 'rip' refers to the act of copying a file from a CD to a computer. When you copy files from a computer to a CD, you 'burn' them to CD.

! ALERT: Make sure you insert an audio CD into your disk drive. When you insert a blank recordable CD, you see pop-up boxes and you'll need to close them if you want to use Windows Media Player to copy your files.

Get started with Windows Media Center

Media Center is a Windows 7 application that lets you play and organise a wider range of media than Media Player, including live television. By now you're probably getting the hang of how to find and open this and other Windows applications: just go to the Start menu.

1 Click Start.

2 Type Media Center.

3 Click Windows Media Center.

4 To set up Media Center the first time, accept the defaults.

ALERT: You won't be able to watch live TV if you don't have a TV tuner installed.

? DID YOU KNOW?

Media Center's interface includes several menus: Tasks, Pictures + Videos, Movies, Music, Sports and Extras.

! ALERT: You have to type the US spelling of 'center' when you open this program.

Watch live TV

I just hate it when I miss my favourite TV shows. Now I'm good to go no matter what's on that night. Here's how to be a couch potato even if you're away from your couch. Media Center helps you watch TV, either on the Internet or on live television.

1 Open Media Center.

2 If necessary, under TV, click live tv setup.

3 Once you have set up your TV, move once to the right of recorded TV and click live TV.

4 Position the mouse at the bottom of the live TV screen to show the controls you need.

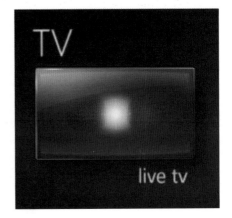

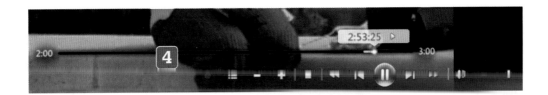

HOT TIP: If you don't have TV tuner hardware at hand, keep in mind that many television networks archive recent episodes of their most popular programmes on their websites so you can view them any time, using programs such as Media Player.

HOT TIP: If you receive an error when you click live TV, either you don't have the television signal properly set up or you don't have a TV tuner. Many come with antennas or you can find them for as little as £14.99 at Amazon.co.uk.

DID YOU KNOW?
There are lots of ways to navigate the Media Center. You can use the mouse, the arrow keys on the keyboard or a remote control.

Watch Internet TV

If you're curious about the sort of televised entertainment you can watch with your computer and you haven't yet purchased a TV tuner add-on, you can watch a growing selection of Internet TV using Media Center as your guide.

1 Under Extras click internet tv.

2 Click Install to get started.

3 Pass your mouse over the episodes and scroll through different options.

4 Double-click a TV show to watch it.

ALERT: You need to be connected to the Internet before you try to watch Internet TV. You also need a high-speed connection such as a cable or DSL line to view TV without delays.

? DID YOU KNOW?

If you have a TV tuner connected to your computer, you can use a handheld controller to play TV and move from one programme to another.

Pause and rewind live TV

The hand that controls the remote control at home belongs to the person who rules the world. With Media Center on your computer, it's all at your fingertips as well.

1 Open Media Center.

2 Click Live TV.

3 Locate a show you want to watch using the controls at the bottom of the screen. The + and – signs on the left change the channels up or down.

4 Click the double vertical lines to pause the programme.

5 Click fast-forward or rewind to move back or forward through the programme.

 HOT TIP: Pass your mouse over the contents of the Media Center window in order to see controls. When you pass your mouse pointer close to the right or left edge of the window, navigation arrows appear. When you pass your mouse over the bottom right corner of the window, the stop, play, back, forward and other controls appear.

 HOT TIP: Recorded TV is also an option with Media Player. If you record a TV show digitally and save it on a disk connected to your computer, you can use Media Center to play it.

 DID YOU KNOW?
To fast-forward through the commercials, press pause at the beginning of the show. For a 30-minute show, pause for 10 minutes; for a 60-minute show, pause for 20 minutes.

Obtain programme schedules

As you can probably guess, you'll get the Program Info screen when you click on Program Info. Then you can record a single programme or a series, plus you'll have access to more information about the show. Here's how to obtain programme schedules.

1 Open Media Center.

2 Under TV, click Guide.

3 Hover the mouse over any show in the Guide to see programme information.

4 Click the show one time to view additional information.

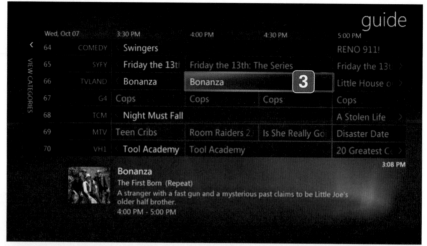

Record a TV show

You have to tell Media Center what shows you want to record. You can record a show once or configure a series recording.

1 Locate the show to record in the Guide.

2 Right-click the title and choose Record or Record Series.

3 Once a show is scheduled to record, you can change record settings. Right-click and choose Series info.

4 Click Series Settings, if applicable.

5 Change the settings as desired.

6 Click Save.

HOT TIP: When you record a series with the defaults you record new shows and reruns. Make sure you know what's going to happen!

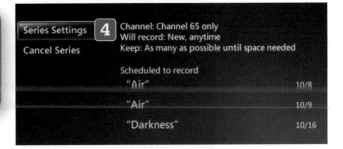

Watch a recorded TV show

Once you've recorded some TV, you can watch what you have stored.

1 Click TV.

2 Click recorded TV.

3 Double-click the show to play it.

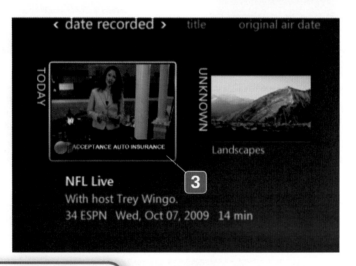

Play a DVD

One of the most common uses you'll have for your computer is playing movies on DVD. You can play your disk using Windows Media Center or Windows Media Player. Windows Media Player is designed to start automatically.

1 Put a DVD in your computer's DVD drive.

2 If prompted, choose play DVD using Windows Media Center. (You will probably not be prompted.)

3 Use the controls at the bottom of the screen to pause, stop, rewind and fast-forward.

4 Click Play all or one of the other options to play the DVD.

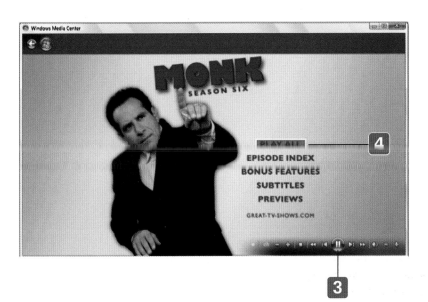

? **DID YOU KNOW?**

You can also browse to Movies in Media Center and from the submenus choose Play DVD.

HOT TIP: If you use Media Center, you can press fast-forward to skip the previews before the main feature. I find this doesn't always work with Media Player.

12 Keep your computer secure

Introduction

Even if you don't know a great deal about computers, you are probably familiar with terms like 'hacker' and 'computer virus'. When you connect your computer to the Internet or when you download software, you open yourself up to risks. In some cases, danger may come in the form of a piece of software that 'spies' on your files or your keystrokes, or that might even try to take over your computer so it can be used to attack a website. Your personal security may also be threatened by a curious family member.

The good news is that by observing a few common-sense practices and by installing one or two security programs, you can avoid having your privacy and your computer compromised. Just keep an eye out for security warnings so you can resolve them. In the meantime, the built-in features and other available safeguards are there to keep you and your data safe.

Adjust User Account Control

For an extra measure of protection, Windows provides you with a feature called User Account Control. It prompts you to verify that you want to launch an application or perform a task that could involve computer security. If you're sure no unauthorised users will have access to your computer, you may want to disable this feature. To disable User Account Control, follow these steps.

1. Click Start and in the Start Search window type User Account Control.

2. In the results, click Change User Account Control settings.

3. Move the slider to the appropriate setting.

4. Click OK.

5. Click Yes to verify the change.

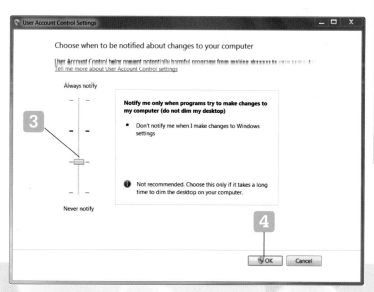

? **DID YOU KNOW?**
It's really just an extra click now and again. It's best to leave the default settings.

Hide a file or folder

One way to protect sensitive documents and data from unauthorised use is to designate it as 'hidden'. Hidden files can't be seen in Windows Explorer or My Computer.

1 Click Start.

2 Click your name in the Start menu to open your personal folder.

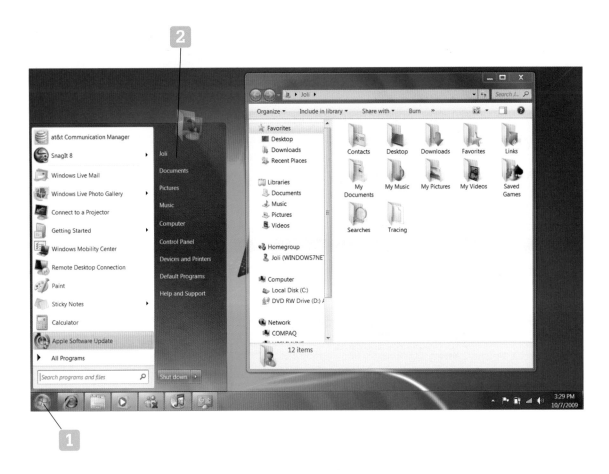

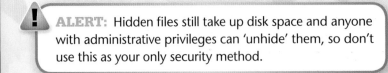

ALERT: Hidden files still take up disk space and anyone with administrative privileges can 'unhide' them, so don't use this as your only security method.

3 Right-click the file or folder you want to hide and choose Properties from the context menu.

4 Click Hidden.

5 Click OK.

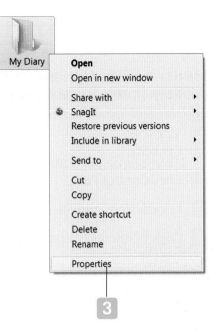

My Diary

| Open |
| Open in new window |
| Share with ▶ |
| SnagIt ▶ |
| Restore previous versions |
| Include in library ▶ |
| Send to ▶ |
| Cut |
| Copy |
| Create shortcut |
| Delete |
| Rename |
| Properties |

3

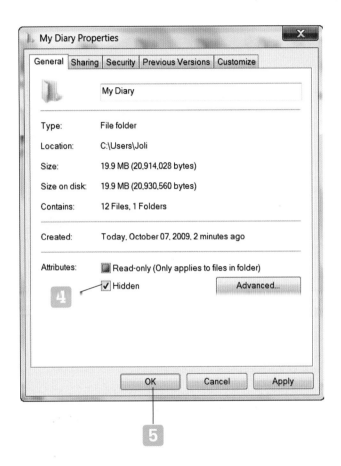

My Diary Properties

General | Sharing | Security | Previous Versions | Customize

My Diary

Type: File folder
Location: C:\Users\Joli
Size: 19.9 MB (20,914,028 bytes)
Size on disk: 19.9 MB (20,930,560 bytes)
Contains: 12 Files, 1 Folders
Created: Today, October 07, 2009, 2 minutes ago

Attributes: ☐ Read-only (Only applies to files in folder)
               4 ☑ Hidden   Advanced...

OK | Cancel | Apply

5

🔥 **HOT TIP:** The more advanced versions of Windows give you the ability to encrypt files and folders. Open the Properties dialogue box for the file or folder you want to protect, click Advanced; if the option to encrypt the item is available, tick and click OK.

Set up Windows Update

Security is a moving target, with new patches and features appearing all the time. If Windows Update is enabled and configured properly, Windows 7 will check for security updates and install them automatically.

1 Click Start.

2 Click Control Panel.

3 Click System and Security.

4 Click Windows Update.

Windows Update
Turn automatic updating on or off | Check for updates | View installed updates **4**

5 In the left pane, click Change settings.

6 Configure the settings as shown on this page.

7 Click OK.

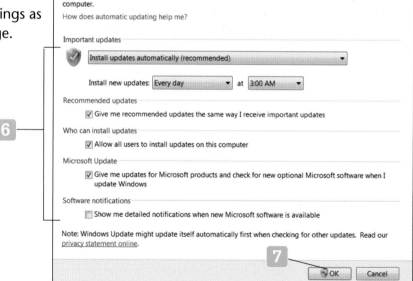

Choose how Windows can install updates

When your computer is online, Windows can automatically check for important updates and install them using these settings. When new updates are available, you can also install them before shutting down the computer.

How does automatic updating help me?

Important updates

Install updates automatically (recommended)

Install new updates: Every day   at 3:00 AM

Recommended updates

☑ Give me recommended updates the same way I receive important updates

Who can install updates

☑ Allow all users to install updates on this computer

Microsoft Update

☑ Give me updates for Microsoft products and check for new optional Microsoft software when I update Windows

Software notifications

☐ Show me detailed notifications when new Microsoft software is available

Note: Windows Update might update itself automatically first when checking for other updates. Read our privacy statement online.

7

OK | Cancel

 HOT TIP: Some updates will be installed automatically, but others are optional. You can view them and install them yourself if you wish.

 DID YOU KNOW?
Even if updates are installed automatically, you should check that the recommended settings are enabled correctly. You should also occasionally check manually for optional updates.

Clear out malware with Windows Defender

Most of the time you can be secure in the knowledge that Windows Defender, which is enabled by default and runs in the background, is protecting your computer from online threats such as hackers. If you're worried, however, you can run a manual scan. That is important if you suspect that your computer has been attacked by malware (a virus, worm or spyware).

1 Click Start and in the Start search window, type Windows Defender.

2 Click Windows Defender in the results.

3 Click the arrow next to Scan.

4 Select the desired scan type.

5 When the scan is done, click the X in the top right corner to close the Windows Defender window.

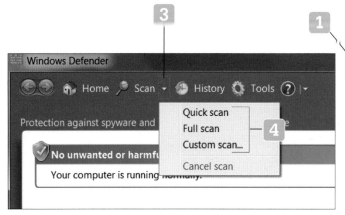

HOT TIP: Click Full scan to scan your entire computer. When you click Quick scan, the scan does not include all of your resources.

HOT TIP: Click Full scan if you think the entire contents of your computer have been infected.

Use the Action Center

The Action Center is an important tool for keeping your computer running smoothly. You can use it to view and resolve problems that occur on your computer, as well as fix security holes.

1 Click the Action Center icon on the taskbar. It's the one that looks like a flag.

2 Click Open Action Center.

3 Check the security settings for your computer. You may see amber, red or green items.

4 Click Check for solutions for any item to view its resolution.

5 If desired, perform the steps to resolve the problem.

ALERT: A red banner in the Security Center means an item is not up to date and your computer could be compromised. An amber banner means there are some issues and you are not fully protected. A green banner means the item is up to date and protecting your system.

Enable Windows Firewall

Fairy tales are full of situations where aspiring young princes must discover the right word or action to enter the magic kingdom. Firewalls are kind of like that. Whether the data is coming from the Internet or from a local network, the firewall decides whether it's good enough to be granted entry. Bad data will be blocked from your computer.

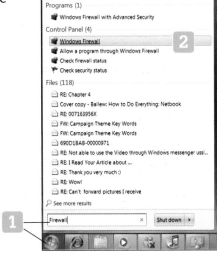

1   Click Start, and in the Start Search window type Firewall.

2   Click Windows Firewall in the results.

3   Under Windows Firewall, click Turn Windows Firewall on or off.

4   Verify that the firewall is turned on and that the other settings are OK.

5   Click OK.

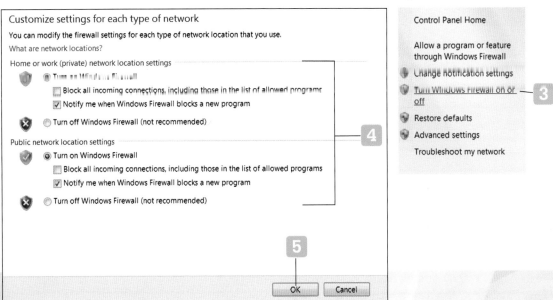

?   DID YOU KNOW?

You obviously need your firewall turned on to stop hackers from gaining access to your computer. But this safeguard will also help prevent your computer from unknowingly being infected by a virus or used by a hacker to send out malicious code.

Handle Action Center warnings

Your Action Center keeps you in the know. It will tell you if your antivirus software is out of date or not installed, if you don't have the proper security settings configured, or if Windows Update or the firewall is disabled. You need to open the Action Center occasionally to view the status of your PC.

1 Click the Action Center icon in the taskbar.

2 Read the warnings and see if there are any messages.

3 If you see a message or problem you would like to read or address, click it.

4 As detailed in the section Use the Action Center, resolve problems as desired.

HOT TIP: Don't apply the attitude that if you ignore something it will go away. Pay attention to alerts and take care of problems promptly.

DID YOU KNOW?

Windows 7 comes with malware protection. However, you need to install anti-virus software yourself so that your computer will be protected from viruses and worms.

5 To view more or less Action Center warnings and alerts, click Change Action Center settings.

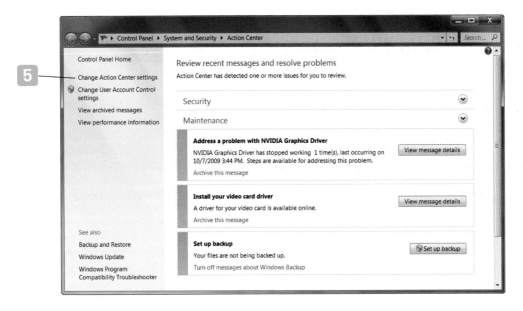

6 Deselect what you no longer want to receive information and alerts for.

7 Click OK.

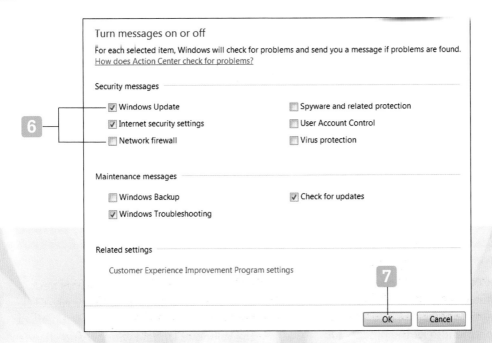

Run Windows Update

It's good to have faith in the system, but it's also good to take matters into your own hands. Sometimes you have reason to be suspicious. Other times it's good to perform regular maintenance and upkeep. Here's how to run a manual update.

1 Click Start, click All Programs and click Windows Update.

2 Click Check for updates. Wait while the process completes.

Control Panel Home

Check for updates 2

Change settings

View update history

Restore hidden updates

Updates: frequently asked questions

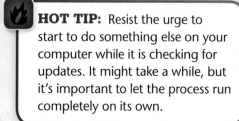

HOT TIP: Resist the urge to start to do something else on your computer while it is checking for updates. It might take a while, but it's important to let the process run completely on its own.

? DID YOU KNOW?

Windows Update is configured to check for and install updates automatically. Click the Change settings link in the left pane of the Windows Update window and change the default settings.

3 If updates exist, even optional ones, click to view them.

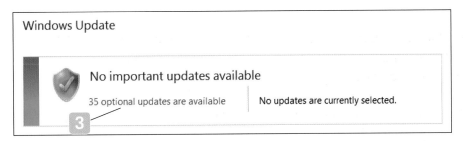

4 Some optional updates will need to be installed; some not. All critical and security related updates should be installed.

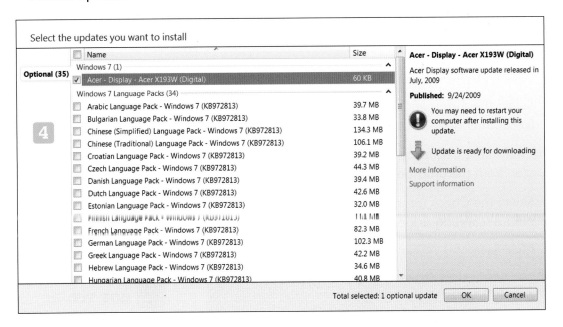

5 Restart your PC if prompted.

⚠️ **ALERT:** If you set Windows Update to run automatically, you might find your computer restarting automatically to finish the update installation sequence. You may get a pop-up warning, but even so it's best to save frequently so nothing gets lost.

Configure Windows Defender to run automatically

When you hear the word 'scan' you might think 'photos'. But if the subject is security, it refers to searching your computer for problem files as part of the process of detecting spyware. Configuring Windows Defender to run automatically gives you one less thing to worry about in your busy life.

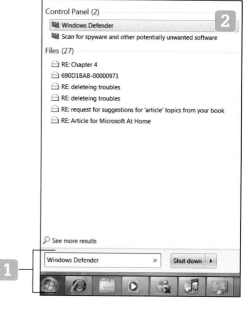

1 Click Start, and in the Start Search box type Windows Defender (or Defender).

2 Click Windows Defender in the results.

3 Click Tools.

4 Click Options.

5 Select the Automatically scan my computer (recommended) tick box.

6 Choose the frequency, time of day and type of scan from the drop-down lists.

7 Select the Check for updated definitions before scanning tick box.

8 Click Save.

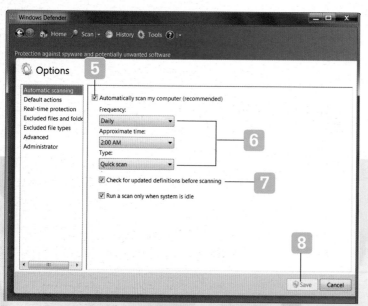

HOT TIP: To exclude files or locations from the regular scans, use the Advanced Options in the Windows Defender dialogue box. Click the Add button and browse for the location or file you want to exclude.

13 Maintain your computer in top shape

Introduction

Like anything else, your computer requires a little maintenance and upkeep. By taking a few simple steps on a periodic basis, you will be able to keep your computer running in top shape. You'll also avoid trouble; you won't encounter files or programs that open slowly and your hard disk won't get clogged with data so that it is difficult to navigate. Look on this chapter as a sort of weekly cleaning and upkeep routine for your computer that will keep it operating for years to come.

Select a Power Plan

Windows 7 offers three distinct power plans that allow you to easily maximise a laptop's battery life, put a desktop PC to sleep when it's not being used and to save electricity. By default, the selected power plan is Balanced but Power Saver and High Performance are available. When running a laptop on its battery, choose Power Saver. When using a computer for gaming or other tasks that require all of the computer's resources, choose High Performance.

To select a power plan:

1 Click Start and type Power.

2 In the results list, click Choose a power plan.

3 From the Power Options window, select a plan.

4 Reduce the screen brightness to save even more energy.

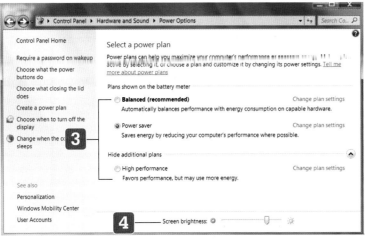

? DID YOU KNOW?

You can click Change plan settings to see and change features of any plan, like how long the computer should be idle before going to sleep. (Remember to click Save changes if you make changes here.)

🔥 HOT TIP: You don't have to click Next, Save or OK after selecting a plan – simply close the window.

Manage battery power use

In the previous tasks, you learned some behaviours that will help conserve battery power. Your laptop also has battery power routines that you can adjust. Preconfigured power schemes will help you manage your battery life.

1 Click Start.

2 Click Control Panel.

3 Click Hardware and Sound.

4 Click Power Options.

5 Click one of the power schemes, such as Power saver, which will maximise battery life.

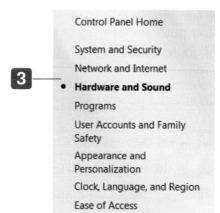

Control Panel Home

System and Security

Network and Internet

3 — • **Hardware and Sound**

Programs

User Accounts and Family Safety

Appearance and Personalization

Clock, Language, and Region

Ease of Access

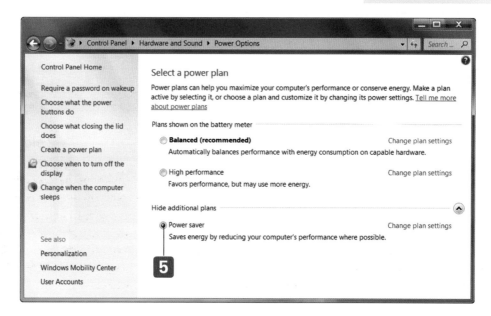

Control Panel Home

Require a password on wakeup

Choose what the power buttons do

Choose what closing the lid does

Create a power plan

Choose when to turn off the display

Change when the computer sleeps

See also

Personalization

Windows Mobility Center

User Accounts

Select a power plan

Power plans can help you maximize your computer's performance or conserve energy. Make a plan active by selecting it, or choose a plan and customize it by changing its power settings. Tell me more about power plans

Plans shown on the battery meter

○ **Balanced (recommended)**   Change plan settings
   Automatically balances performance with energy consumption on capable hardware.

○ High performance   Change plan settings
   Favors performance, but may use more energy.

Hide additional plans

● Power saver   Change plan settings
   Saves energy by reducing your computer's performance where possible.

ALERT: Keep in mind that there are tradeoffs with power schemes – the routine that gives you the longest battery life will also cause your laptop to go to sleep the quickest when you're not using it.

HOT TIP: In the Power Options window you can also choose what happens when you close a laptop's lid, change what the power buttons do, and even create your own customised power plan.

Keep your battery charged

Just like you used to wind your wristwatch, if your computer is a laptop now you charge your battery. You do the charging not by removing the battery and plugging it into a special charging device but by keeping it in your laptop and plugging your laptop into the power mains using your AC/DC adapter.

1 Connect the AC/DC adapter to the laptop.

2 Connect the adapter to the mains socket.

3 Turn the laptop on, if necessary.

4 Check the power meter icon in the taskbar to make sure the laptop is plugged in. If your laptop is plugged in and charging, the icon will appear with a plug, as shown below.

5 If your laptop is on battery power you'll see the icon below.

 HOT TIP: You can also track the amount of battery power remaining and whether or not the battery is charging, in Windows Mobility Center.

? DID YOU KNOW?
Your laptop battery will charge up whether you are working on it or not and whether it is switched on or off. However, it will charge more quickly if it is switched off.

 ALERT: As stated in Chapter 1, it's better to plug your laptop into a surge protector rather than directly into the mains, to protect the device from power surges.

Uninstall programs you don't need

You probably have programs installed on your computer that you'll never use. To save disk space and to keep any programs from running in the background without your knowledge, uninstall them as follows.

1 Open the Control Panel.

2 Click Programs.

3 Under Programs, click Uninstall a program.

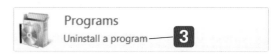

Programs
Uninstall a program —— **3**

4 Scan the list of installed applications and select the one you want to remove.

5 Click Uninstall.

6 Click Yes when prompted.

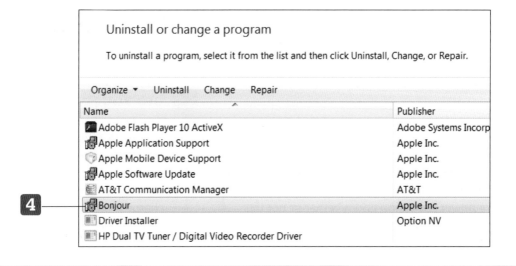

Uninstall or change a program

To uninstall a program, select it from the list and then click Uninstall, Change, or Repair.

Organize ▾   Uninstall   Change   Repair

Name	Publisher
Adobe Flash Player 10 ActiveX	Adobe Systems Incorp
Apple Application Support	Apple Inc.
Apple Mobile Device Support	Apple Inc.
Apple Software Update	Apple Inc.
AT&T Communication Manager	AT&T
Bonjour	Apple Inc.
Driver Installer	Option NV
HP Dual TV Tuner / Digital Video Recorder Driver	

4

 HOT TIP: When you select a program to install you may see two options: Uninstall and Change. If you see the Change option, you can click it to add or remove program applications. For instance, you could remove Microsoft Office Access and Excel, but keep Microsoft Office Word and PowerPoint.

Back up your files

One of the many benefits of using Windows 7 is the presence of safeguards that keep you from losing data in case your system suddenly stops working (or in the language of computers, 'crashes'). Nevertheless, it's always a good idea to back up your files. You learned how to do so in preceding chapters by dragging files to an external drive. You can also use Windows' own Backup and Restore.

1 Click Start, and click Control Panel.

2 Under System and Security, click Back up your computer.

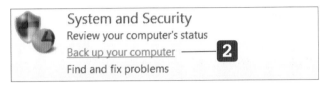

3 Click Set up backup. (If you don't see this but instead see something else, you've already run the Backup process at least once.)

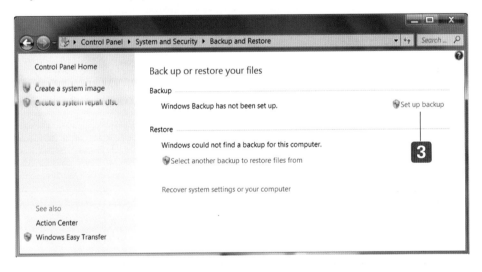

SEE ALSO: See Restore files, the next section, for more on using System Backup and Restore to replace files you may have lost.

4 Select the location where you want to back up your files.

5 Click Next.

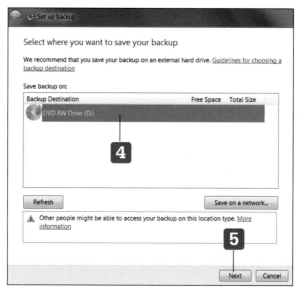

6 Click Let Windows choose (recommended) and click Next.

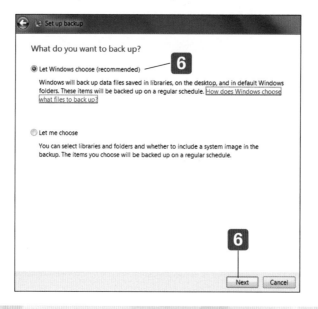

7 Follow any remaining prompts (e.g. to insert a DVD), if applicable.

8 Accept the default settings and click Save settings and run backup.

Save settings and run backup

9 Wait while the backup completes.

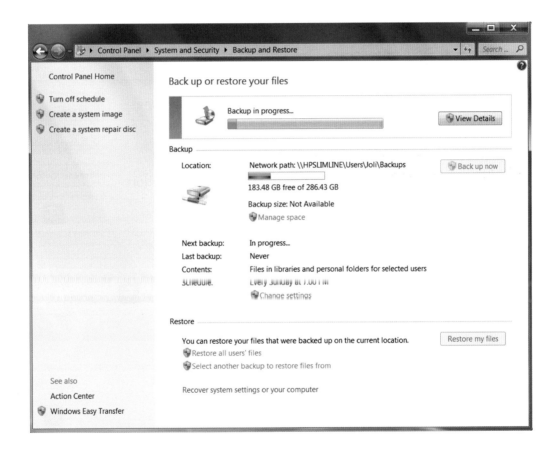

Restore files

In the best of all possible worlds, you'll never have to restore files, because you won't have computer crashes or other problems. But such problems can and do occur and it's best to be prepared. If the need arises, it's possible to do the following using the files you backed up earlier with Backup and Restore.

1 Open Backup and Restore.

2 Click Restore my files.

3 Click Browse for folders to locate the backup folder.

4 Select the desired backup, noting there may be more than one, and click Add folder.

5 Click the folder you just added, and click Next.

6 Make a selection. Either restore the files to their original location or a new location. Click Restore.

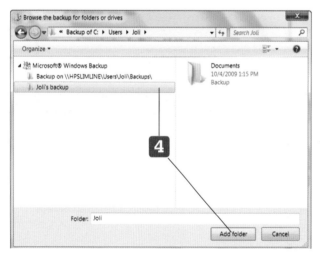

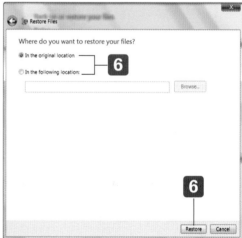

 HOT TIP: As you might expect, you can click Start, type Backup and Restore and press Enter to open this Windows application.

⚠ ALERT: If you are not sure whether you want to restore over existing files – for instance, if you aren't sure the existing files are actually older than the ones you are restoring from a backup – by all means restore in a different location, even if it is a folder you create on your file system.

Clean up your hard disk

As you work and surf the Internet, your hard disk compiles lots of files you don't need, and don't even know you have. For instance, website images and text files are stored in an area of your disk called disk cache so the same sites can appear more quickly on subsequent visits. You can use Windows' Disk Cleanup routine to delete such files.

1 Click Start and in the Start Search window type Disk Cleanup.

2 Click Disk Cleanup in the results.

3 Wait while the initial scan of your computer completes.

4 Tick the boxes next to the items you want to delete.

5 Click OK to start the cleanup.

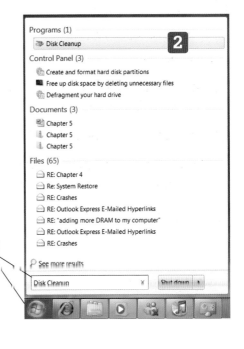

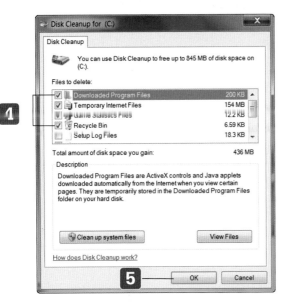

? DID YOU KNOW?
You don't need temporary internet files, especially if you have a high-speed Internet connection. The temporary files save only a few seconds when you revisit a website.

🔥 HOT TIP: The cleanup routine can take several minutes, so perform this task when you don't need your computer for other purposes.

Clean your computer

There is the nice feeling of having your possessions squeaky clean. But computers really can be harmed by dust, dirt and food particles. You'll want to give attention to external ports and the keyboard, as well as to the case itself.

1 Click Start.

2 Click the arrow shown at the bottom of the Start menu.

3 Click Shut down.

4 Unplug the computer from the wall outlet.

5 Disconnect all external hardware (e.g. webcams, flash drives, printers).

6 Use a vacuum cleaner with a small attachment to pull dust from the external ports. If there is an air intake, clean that as well.

7 Use compressed air to blow out remaining dust and dirt.

8 Clean any additional crevices with a dry cotton swab.

9 Clean the plastic outside the tower with a cotton rag sprayed with a mild, non-abrasive cleaner.

10 Reconnect the peripherals.

 HOT TIP: If you're challenged by a particularly sticky spot, add a touch of vinegar to the cloth along with a mild, non-abrasive cleaner. Just keep in mind that you really do not want to get any electrical parts or ports wet.

 DID YOU KNOW?

Two to three times a year is typically the goal for cleaning. But don't hesitate to sanitise more often if someone has a cold, your cat sheds a lot or you snack on crumbly food while using your computer.

Use a surge protector

While it's sad to have to replace a refrigerator or television because of a power surge, it's even more of a disaster if you lose data on your computer you haven't had a chance to back up yet. To be doubly safe, use surge protectors and back up often.

1 Purchase a surge protector.

2 Plug in your computer.

3 Plug in other computer hardware, such as modems and printers.

 DID YOU KNOW?

When the voltage from an electrical current unexpectedly increases, there is the potential for damaging sensitive electrical equipment. In the case of your computer, both the power supply and the internal parts are at risk during lightning storms or surges caused by blasts from personal generators or a city's over-taxed electrical grid. It could even be a problem if a tree trimmer or power company worker touches the electrical transformer.

 HOT TIP: As you might expect, you can use the Start menu to open Windows Update quickly. Click Start, type update, and click Windows Update when it appears in the Start menu.

 HOT TIP: Surge protectors can also function as a power strip by providing additional electrical outlets. Make sure what you buy is actually a surge protector and not just a power strip, however. A plain old power strip won't provide any protection from an electrical surge.

Defragment your hard disk

Defragmenting sounds bad, but it actually reassembles data on your hard drive to use the space more efficiently. It's necessary because your computer stores bits of any file you save in more than one place. Disk Defragmenter runs by default on a schedule, but you can run it if you want to. At the very least, you can verify it's set to run automatically.

1 Click Start, and in the Start Search window type Defrag.

2 Click Disk Defragmenter.

3 Click Defragment disk, if desired. Note you can also click Analyze disk to find out if the process is actually needed.

4 When the process is complete, click Close (the X in the upper right) to close the window.

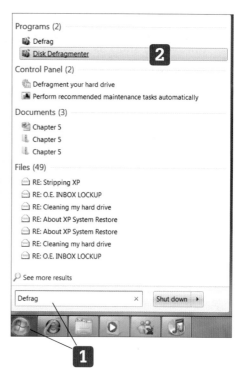

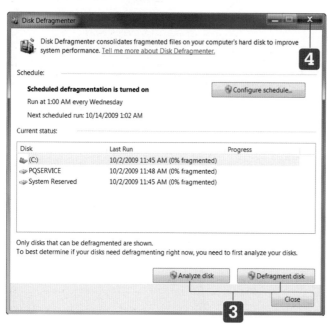

? **DID YOU KNOW?**

Windows will show you a progress window, but the process can take several hours. It might speed things up a little to turn off energy-saving features such as a screen saver.

HOT TIP: Click Configure schedule to change when the Disk Defragmenter runs by default.

Delete cookies your browser gathers

If you're at the bakery, the more cookies the better. But cookies on your computer can pile up and take over valuable space. They also can represent an invasion of privacy. Here's how to get rid of them.

1 Click the Internet Explorer icon on the taskbar.

2 From the Internet Explorer menu bar, choose Safety and Delete Browsing History.

3 Select what to delete. Note there's an explanation beside each option.

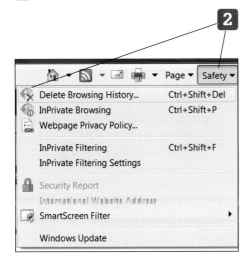

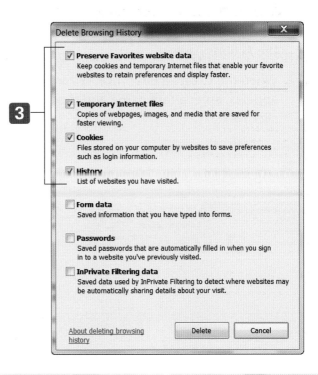

 HOT TIP: If you change your privacy to a higher setting, fewer Internet businesses will be able to place cookies on your computer when you visit their sites.

 DID YOU KNOW?
Pop-up windows may appear because of cookies. You might get suggestions for items to buy online. They might greet you by name when you return to a site because they have stored your membership information.

Remind yourself about maintenance tasks

If you set alarms on every electronic device you own, you can program your computer to remind you to perform regular maintenance tasks. The Task Scheduler will then periodically display a message.

1 Click Start, click Control Panel, click System and Security, then click Schedule tasks under Administrative Tools.

2 When the Task Scheduler dialogue box appears, click the Create Basic Task link in the Actions pane.

3 When the Create a Basic Task Wizard dialogue box appears, enter a task name and description and click Next.

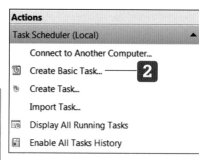

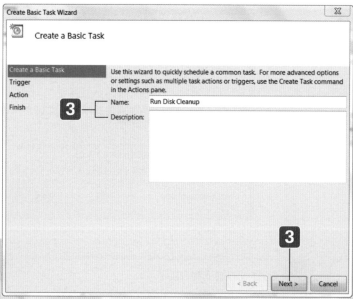

ALERT: Don't get too creative with messages to yourself. It will probably be adequate to say: Run a Disk Cleanup Soon?

4 In the Task Trigger window that appears, choose when to run the task.

5 Click Next. In the next wizard window that appears, choose a criterion from the Start drop-down list and use the Settings to specify how often to perform the task and when and at what time of day to begin.

6 In the Action window that appears, select Display a Message and then click Next.

7 In the Display a Message window that appears, enter the title and contents of the message you want to appear.

8 Click Next and review the information in the Summary window that appears.

9 Click Finish and then click the Close button.

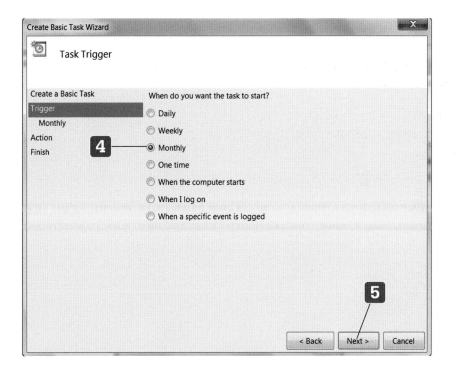

HOT TIP: Maintenance is good, but you don't need to go overboard. Once a month is usually more than adequate for most system maintenance tasks.

Top 10 Computer Problems Solved

Introduction

Nobody likes technical difficulties, but they happen. One of the nice features about Windows is that, as the operating system grows more advanced, the tools and options for getting out of trouble grow more powerful as well as easier to use. Knowing the solutions that are available to you and how to use them will, I hope, dilute some of the stress involved when you encounter computer problems.

Problem 1: Windows isn't working properly – how will using System Restore fix this?

System Restore is enabled by default. To protect your computer from harm, System Restore will create and save restore points that contain information about your computer that Windows uses to work properly. If you're about to do something that has the potential to cause your computer harm, you can create a restore point manually by clicking Create. You should check to make sure System Restore is enabled.

1. Click Start, and right-click Computer.

2. Click Properties.

3. Click System protection.

4. Click the C: drive, or the System drive.

5. Verify that System Restore protection is On.

6. Click Configure.

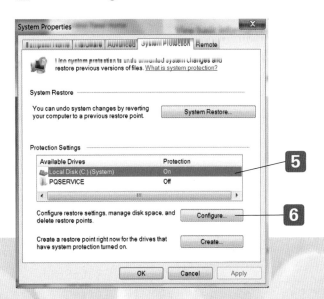

ALERT: You can create a System Restore point right now by clicking Create in the System Properties window, under the System Protection tab.

7 Move the slider so that System Restore has about 1 GB of space to use. (Provided you have ample disk space.)

8 Click OK, and OK again to close the windows.

Now, you can use System Restore.

9 Click Start, and type System Restore in the Start Search window.

10 From the results click System Restore.

11 Accept the recommended restore point, if you believe that's about the time the problem occurred. Otherwise, click Choose a different restore point and select one.

12 Click Next.

13 Click Finish, and let System Restore complete. Your computer will restart.

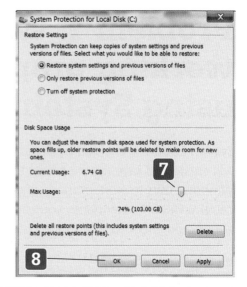

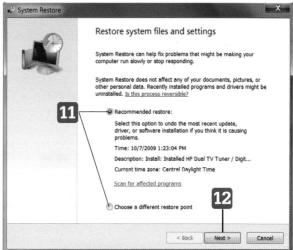

 SEE ALSO: In order to restore your files, System Restore needs to have taken a snapshot of your operating system at some time in the past.

 ALERT: If you're using a laptop, make sure it's plugged in. You don't want System Restore to be interrupted.

 ALERT: Always start with the most recent System Restore point to see if this fixes the problem. If not, use a more distant restore point.

Problem 2: I can't connect to the Internet

Sooner or later, you'll probably encounter problems connecting to the Internet. Before you call your ISP's support staff, there are some tried-and-tested approaches you should take.

1 Make sure your modem, router, cables and other hardware are properly connected, plugged in and turned on.

2 If your computer uses a wireless connection to get online, restart your computer.

3 Open the Network and Sharing Center.

4 Click the red X.

5 Perform the steps presented in the Windows Network Diagnostics dialogue box.

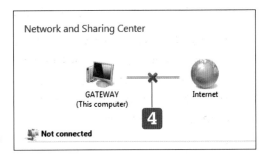

Network and Sharing Center

GATEWAY
(This computer)

Internet

4

Not connected

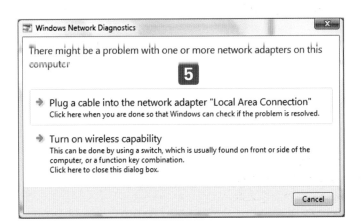

Windows Network Diagnostics

There might be a problem with one or more network adapters on this computer

5

→ Plug a cable into the network adapter "Local Area Connection"
Click here when you are done so that Windows can check if the problem is resolved.

→ Turn on wireless capability
This can be done by using a switch, which is usually found on front or side of the computer, or a function key combination.
Click here to close this dialog box.

Cancel

! ALERT: When restarting a cable or satellite modem, you need to completely turn it off first. That involves removing any batteries.

? DID YOU KNOW?
You need to turn off all hardware, including the computer, if you're prompted to restart your broadband or satellite connection. Restarting should be done in the following order: cable/satellite/DSL modem, router, computer.

Problem 3: How do I start my computer in Safe Mode?

If your computer doesn't boot up correctly, it could be that an update or program you installed is causing problems. You can use Safe Mode to remove any programs you recently installed to see whether the problem is fixed.

1 Restart by holding down the power button until your computer shuts down, wait a minute, then press it again.

2 Before you see the Windows logo or the progress bar at the bottom of the screen, press and hold the F8 key.

3 From the menu that appears, select Last known good configuration to see whether your computer begins running normally.

4 If step 3 fails, repeat steps 1 and 2.

5 Select Safe Mode. Log in to your computer, if possible.

6 Use Safe Mode to explore your system and remove files or programs that may be causing a problem.

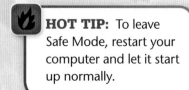
HOT TIP: To leave Safe Mode, restart your computer and let it start up normally.

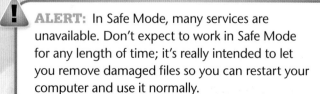
ALERT: In Safe Mode, many services are unavailable. Don't expect to work in Safe Mode for any length of time; it's really intended to let you remove damaged files so you can restart your computer and use it normally.

Problem 4: A device driver I've just installed isn't working properly

You think you're doing a good thing, but you end up worse than you started. But wait. If you download and install a new driver for a piece of hardware and it doesn't work properly, you can use Device Driver Rollback to return to the previously installed driver.

1 Click Start.

2 Right-click Computer and click Properties.

3 Under Tasks, click Device Manager.

4 Click the + sign next to the hardware that uses the driver you want to roll back and double-click the device name.

5 Click the Driver tab and click Roll Back Driver.

6 Click OK and restart if necessary.

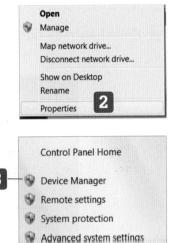

DID YOU KNOW?
The Roll Back Driver option will be available only if a new driver has recently been installed. You can only roll back to the previous driver.

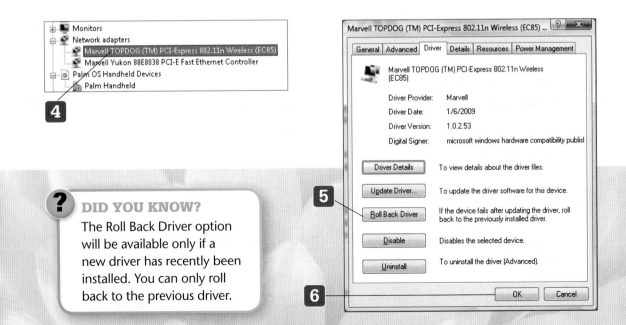

Problem 5: My hardware isn't working

It's so obvious, but yet so easy to miss. Your mouse or its wireless component needs to be plugged in. Your cable modem needs to be securely connected to the laptop and the wall outlet. When troubleshooting, check that first.

1 Locate the hardware device that isn't working.

2 If a connection is necessary, follow the cord to make sure it is securely plugged in.

3 If the hardware doesn't begin to work within a few seconds, restart.

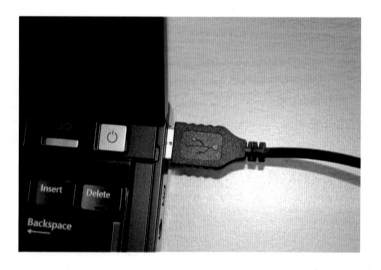

 DID YOU KNOW?

Maybe it's just as sensible to believe in fairy dust, but often you can fix the problem simply by removing a cable and reinserting it.

 HOT TIP: Many bits of hardware have multiple connections and connection types. If one type of connection doesn't work, try another. For example, go for FireWire instead of USB.

Problem 6: Why won't my computer start up?

If you have a desktop computer, try connecting and reconnecting the power cord. If you have a laptop, you need to plug it in and recharge the batteries, locate the power button, insert the battery and view the battery status.

1 Connect the battery by doing the following: carefully turn the laptop upside down and place it on a desk or table, locate the battery bay and open it, unlatch the battery latch, install the battery, lock the battery into place, secure the latch and close the battery bay door.

2 Locate the power cord, which may consist of two pieces that need to be connected.

3 Connect the power cord to the back or side of the computer.

4 Plug the power cord into the power mains.

5 Open the laptop's lid (if applicable) and press the Power button.

6 Open Mobility Center. (Click Start and in the Start Search window type Mobility.)

7 Click the arrow to view the three power plans: Balanced, Power saver and High performance. Pick one.

8 View the current status of the battery life.

 HOT TIP: If your computer won't start at all after you have plugged it into several different outlets, try a new power cord if you have one or can borrow one from a friend's computer.

 ALERT: If your computer does not start up after you have changed power outlets and power cords, you should take it into a service centre. The power supply inside the computer may need to be replaced.

Problem 7: How do I cut down on junk email (spam)?

Some spam is annoying and some is downright offensive. Here's how to get less of what you don't want by enabling the junk email filter in Windows Live Mail.

1 If Windows Live Mail detects an email message that is potentially harmful and it displays a dialogue box like this, click Junk E-mail Options.

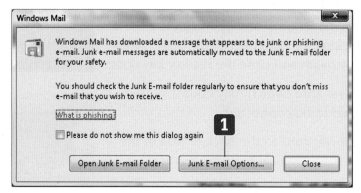

2 If you want to manually adjust junk mail settings, click the Menu icon and click Safety options.

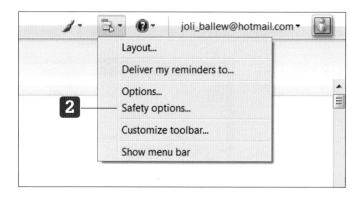

? **DID YOU KNOW?**

In regard to the Options tab, it makes the most sense to select Low for starters. You can always move it up to High later if necessary.

3 From the Options tab, make a selection.

4 Click the Phishing tab.

5 Select Protect my Inbox from messages with potential Phishing links.

6 Select Move phishing E-mail to the Junk email folder if you have a pop or IMAP account from your ISP.

7 Click OK.

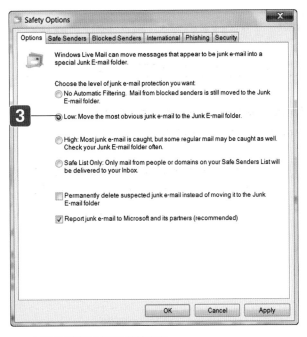

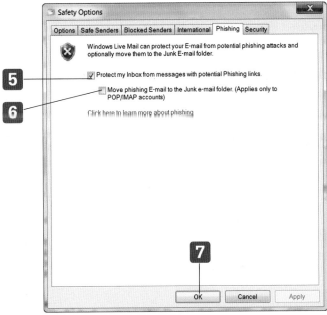

ALERT: 'Phishing' is a harmful practice in which unscrupulous individuals send email messages that attempt to get you to submit personal information such as your credit card numbers in the guise of registering for a service for verifying your identity.

Problem 8: How do I remove programs I don't want?

When you purchase a new computer, it often comes with programs you don't want. You can uninstall these programs in Control Panel.

1 Click Start, and click Control Panel.

2 Click Uninstall a program.

3 Locate the program to uninstall and click Uninstall.

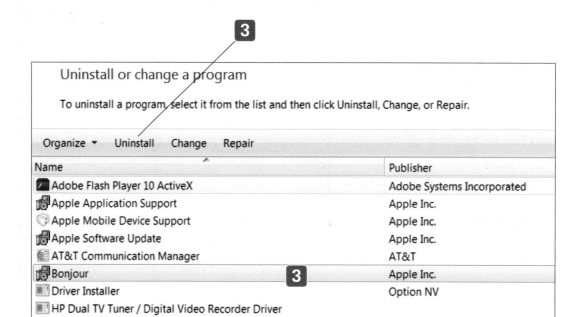

Programs
Uninstall a program ── **2**

3

Uninstall or change a program

To uninstall a program, select it from the list and then click Uninstall, Change, or Repair.

Organize ▾   Uninstall   Change   Repair

Name	Publisher
Adobe Flash Player 10 ActiveX	Adobe Systems Incorporated
Apple Application Support	Apple Inc.
Apple Mobile Device Support	Apple Inc.
Apple Software Update	Apple Inc.
AT&T Communication Manager	AT&T
Bonjour **3**	Apple Inc.
Driver Installer	Option NV
HP Dual TV Tuner / Digital Video Recorder Driver	
iTunes	Apple Inc.

 HOT TIP: You can remove parts of programs when they're in a suite of programs. For instance, you can remove Microsoft Access from Microsoft Office but keep Word and PowerPoint. To do that, click Change.

 HOT TIP: Don't remove programs you don't recognise!

Problem 9: How do I connect to a wireless network when I don't get a notification?

When you get within range of a wireless network, you generally get a pop-up in the Notification area offering the option to connect to it. If you don't see that option, first, check to see if your LAN feature is enabled. Laptops often have switches or a keyboard option to turn on and off Wi-Fi to save battery power. If wireless capabilities are enabled, connect manually.

1 Click the Network icon in the Notification area.

2 Locate the network to connect to and click its name.

3 Click Connect.

4 If prompted, input the security key.

5 If prompted to choose a network type, choose Public if you're in a public place like a coffee shop or library. If you're at home or work, choose Home or Work.

 HOT TIP: Sometimes you have to try twice to connect to a network. If at first you don't succeed, try again!

Problem 10: How do I find my email, messaging and photo-editing programs?

Windows 7 does not come with an email program, a messaging program, or a photo-editing program. There are several options, but the best is to download and install Windows Live Essentials.

1 Click Start.

2 Click Getting Started.

3 Click Get Windows Live Essentials.

4 Follow the directions to complete the installation.

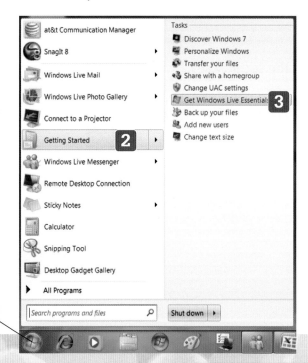

HOT TIP: You'll need a Windows Live ID, so when prompted towards the end of the installation process, make sure to obtain one.

HOT TIP: The Live Essentials suite of applications contains lots of programs. Only get those you know you will use. Mail, Messenger, Photo Gallery and the Toolbar are good choices to start.

USE YOUR COMPUTER WITH CONFIDENCE

9780273723547

9780273723509

9780273723486

9780273723479

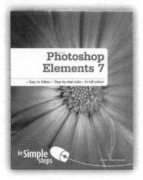

9780273723523

9780273723493

9780273723554

In Simple Steps guides guarantee immediate results. They teach you exactly what you want and need to know on any application; from the most essential tasks to master through to solving the most common problems you'll encounter.

- **Practical** – explains and provides practical solutions to the most commonly encountered problems

- **Easy to understand** – jargon and technical terms explained in simple English

- **Visual** – full colour large screen shots

Practical. Simple. Fast.